Motherlike

Katherine Leyton

Second Story Press

PRAISE FOR *MOTHERLIKE*

"Katherine Leyton writes with the special fury and cutting insight of new motherhood, contending not only with her self-doubt, but interrogating a society that has long attempted to turn women against themselves and make their labors invisible. A hyperintelligent and baring read, delivered with a poet's gift for compression—every line a beating heart—*Motherlike* is both an indictment and a love letter. A beautiful, unflinching, and necessary book."

—Claudia Dey, author of *Daughter, Heartbreaker,* and *Stunt*

"*Motherlike* is an honest, feminist, relatable exploration of the 'deconstruction' of pregnancy and the first 'brilliant, devastating year.' New (and old) urgencies, both personal and political, arise and are amplified in the flurry of nearly-here motherhood. Katherine Leyton examines, with frankness and vulnerability, the question of what makes a (good) mother, and how to be in this flawed and beautiful world."

—Jessica Moore, author of *The Whole Singing Ocean*

Library and Archives Canada Cataloguing in Publication

Title: Motherlike / Katherine Leyton.

Names: Leyton, Katherine, 1983- author.

Identifiers: Canadiana (print) 20230510019 | Canadiana (ebook) 20230510043
 | ISBN 9781772603729 (softcover) | ISBN 9781772603804 (EPUB)

Subjects: LCSH: Leyton, Katherine, 1983- | LCSH: Motherhood. | LCSH:
Motherhood—Social aspects. | LCSH: Mothers—Canada—Biography. |
LCGFT: Autobiographies.

Classification: LCC HQ759 .L49 2024 | DDC 306.874/3—dc23

*Second Story Press gratefully acknowledges the support of the Ontario Arts
Council and the Canada Council for the Arts for our publishing program. We
acknowledge the financial support of the Government of Canada through the
Canada Book Fund.*

Conseil des Arts
du Canada

Canada Council
for the Arts

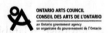

ONTARIO ARTS COUNCIL
CONSEIL DES ARTS DE L'ONTARIO
an Ontario government agency
un organisme du gouvernement de l'Ontario

Funded by the Government of Canada
Financé par le gouvernement du Canada | **Canadä**

Published by
Second Story Press
20 Maud Street, Suite 401
Toronto, ON
M5V 2M5
www.secondstorypress.ca

Notes

The line "I've never seen such devotion in a droid" on page 101 is a quote from
my father, who was inspired by Luke Skywalker's line, "but I've never seen
such devotion in a droid before," in the movie Star Wars: Episode IV—A New
Hope.

P.D. Eastman's story, "Are You My Mother?" inspired the line on 156.

For Jude, Elton, and Ambrose,
and
for my parents

FIRST TRIMESTER

Summer

*One hugely important reason that scholarship,
philosophy, and virtually every other form of public
discourse have been so astonishingly silent on the subject
of motherhood is simply that men do not experience it.
And what we call public discourse is a forum for what
men know.*

—Susan Maushart, *The Mask of Motherhood*

What if I can't transform myself into a mother-person?

—Phyllis Chesler, *With Child: A Diary of
Motherhood*

Two weeks after we conceived you, we went surfing in the California ocean. It was my first time on a surfboard. The ocean was cold, and I got somersaulted under the surface and lost my bearings. I had no sense of whether the ocean floor or the sky was above me.

The water's grip should have been terrifying, but all I felt was a sense of liberation. I was free, for a brief instant, of the nagging sense I must be vigilant with myself.

I am a woman. We are told to keep ourselves safe.

I have this idea my male peers were raised to aspire to motorcycles and roaming the streets, an idea I got from the movies, perhaps. But for us women the message was clear: there's danger everywhere and we are responsible for keeping ourselves out of it. I didn't exactly subscribe to this notion, but I never bought myself a motorcycle and I felt guilty some nights when I lived in Italy and Scotland as a young woman, thinking I might crash into the Atlantic on a plane before my parents ever got to see me again, and this would mean I was a bad daughter—a bad girl.

I had a therapist once who said it seemed like all I wanted was for someone to tell me I was a *good girl.*

Neither your father nor I were able to stand up on our boards and ride a wave that day, but we stood on the beach in our wetsuits after, feeling like we'd accomplished something, thinking that this was it somehow—this was what life was about—a sort of exhilarating swim toward the impossible. We were on our honeymoon.

Swirling under that water—and on that whole trip to California—I didn't know my body contained your fate as well. I drank beer on the flights home. I drank wine in bed in our hotel room the night before we went surfing, listening to the waves crash. I downed tequila and champagne the night I married your father, roughly a week earlier, when you were just a fertilized egg travelling down my fallopian tube.

Before you, I did not know the precise details of what happened in my reproductive system every month. This information was not accorded much significance by my generation's education system or collective consciousness—everyone was just waiting for the sex ed instructor to put the condom on the banana.

I knew an egg was released from my ovaries and if it didn't meet a sperm, would meander into oblivion. Then my uterus would shed itself of blood and the whole thing would start again. Anything beyond that was hazy.

My body, you see, was not for making babies. My body was for sexualizing and displaying, for having sex, for inspecting in the mirror and often hating. Reproduction was for repressing. I started on the pill when I was sixteen, understanding very little about how it worked, except that I could have sex and not become a mother.

My doctor did not even bother to mention to me that the pill might cause a slew of serious side effects. And at that point in time— 1999—doctors did not yet know (or perhaps did not feel comfortable saying) that it could cause depression and mood shifts, despite oral contraceptives being available since the sixties. I am suspicious of why so little research was done on this, even though many women, like my mother, said going on it made them "flat." Or, as the abstract of a 2016 research paper entitled "Association of Hormonal Contraception With Depression" put it:

> Despite the clinical evidence of an influence of hormonal contraception on some women's mood, associations between the use of hormonal contraception and mood disturbances remain inadequately addressed.

Several studies now back up this *clinical evidence*. The data suggests that use of hormonal contraceptives significantly increases a person's risk of depression. In a study published in the American Journal of Psychiatry in 2017, researchers found hormonal contraceptive use doubles the risk of attempted suicide among women and triples the risk of suicide.

I wonder now if being a miserable bitch through my teens and young adulthood was just my nature or if it was an effect of a small plastic package of blue and white pills.

For me, the ritual of those little blue pills made it possible for my boyfriend to come inside me without a condom—a liberty I had absorbed from pop culture as being of the utmost importance.

Meanwhile, my own orgasms with this boyfriend eluded me for nearly four months of sexual activity until he spent a particularly long time going down on me one afternoon. That day, in the presence of a real orgasm, he realized everything before that had been faked.

Two of the researchers who developed the birth control pill, John Rock and Gregory Pincus, tested the drug on patients at the Worcester State Psychiatric Hospital in Massachusetts without their consent, and on poor women in Puerto Rico who were not fully informed of the risks and were often desperate to change their situations. (It should be noted that the trials did adhere to the medical standards of the day, which, from today's vantage point, were highly unethical.)

In the US, from 1960 to 1972, the pill was only legal for married women. In Canada, it was legal for regulating menstruation by 1960, and only became legal for unmarried women for the purpose of preventing pregnancies in 1969.

Early versions of the drug had such high levels of estrogen that women were at unnecessarily high risk of blood clots, stroke, heart attacks, and cancer. It wasn't until medical journalist Barbara Seaman wrote *The Doctors' Case Against the Pill*, and feminists challenged its safety at congressional hearings, that pharmaceutical companies lowered the dose to safer levels—a mere fraction of what they'd originally been.

There are also the dozens of women who died and suffered blood clots after taking the pills Yaz or Yasmin in the 2000s, both developed by Bayer.

And this doesn't even begin to cover the history of other forms of female birth control, like the testing of Depo-Provera—an injectable form of birth control developed by Pfizer—on 14,000 women at the Grady clinic in Atlanta, Georgia, fifty per cent of whom were Black. This testing took place *after* the FDA had refused to approve Depo-Provera due to its link to cancer in laboratory animals. Many of these test subjects did not give their consent to be injected with birth control, and most were not informed of the associated effects, which included not only higher rates of breast, cervical, and uterine cancer, but also severe depression, osteoporosis, and loss of sex drive.

I knew so little about this pill I spent eighteen years putting in my body.

I ran out of my birth control prescription the spring before your father and I married. Instead of booking a doctor's appointment to get a refill, we decided to use the rhythm method until I was ready to get pregnant. We'd been casually discussing trying to have a baby soon but thought we'd wait a little closer to the wedding until we stopped actively attempting to prevent pregnancy. I wanted to be able to drink at the reception.

In July, the month before we got married, we stopped taking precautions. In July, I got pregnant.

I did not expect this. We were trying to take a casual approach, and I thought we'd have months and months to prepare ourselves for the idea of you before you actually happened.

And then by some fluke, there you were.

A few days after your dad and I got home from our honeymoon, I was sitting in a coffee shop and I suddenly just knew about you. My breasts ached and the air was heavy on my skin. My body felt off.

You had been a possibility at the back of my mind because—although I didn't keep close track of my period—I was pretty sure I was late. I'd had a beer at dinner the night before and had hesitated before putting it to my lips.

I left to buy a pregnancy test at the drugstore. I felt like a teenage girl as I paid at the cash, shifty. Even though I was thirty-four, I couldn't possibly be mature enough to have a child and even this cashier knew it.

When I peed on that stick and saw the two lines indicating your existence, I started to tremble and my heart went to my throat.

Nothing could prepare me for the moment I discovered something was growing inside my own body that would become human, a human I would be responsible to and for, for the rest of my life.

I still don't understand how the fucking I've been doing most of my life could produce a small, strong heart that is beating inside me.

Can we pause here?
    A heartbeat.

I am a self-indulgent person.

In my twenties and early thirties, I felt very free, like I did on that surfboard. I lived for myself. I wrote poems even though few people give a fuck about poems. I jumped from job to job. I lived in Rome and Edinburgh and Montreal. I bartended, which means I served people alcohol, acted as their therapist, diffused tense situations, gave lonely, heartbroken souls some respite, worked to lower defenses, then took their money.

Often, I'd go to a bar after my own shift and drink alone. I'd have a bourbon and watch people, eavesdrop on their conversations, drifting briefly into their lives. I didn't want anyone to talk to me. I wanted to listen.

It was my idea of luxury. Women haven't always had the freedom to drink in bars alone.

Sometimes a man would be waiting for me in an apartment somewhere.

Sometimes, I'd return to my roommate, who might be passed out drunk in her bed with the lights and music still blaring.

I was not working toward anything tangible, anything valued. I lived for my own pleasure, my own absurd values.

Do women like that make good mothers? I'd like to know.

After that first positive pregnancy test, which was a generic brand, I went out and bought a brand-name one and peed on that.

I texted a friend: *Two pregnancy tests say I am pregnant.* Predictably, she was somewhat confused: *What?* she replied. I forced myself to be more straightforward: *I think I'm pregnant.*

I hadn't told your father yet. He was at work. I needed to see this written out to see if it could feel true.

I waited for your dad to get home, anxiously pacing the kitchen.

I need to tell you something.

He was startled, then ecstatic. There was life inside me apparently, yours, and we'd made it. It felt like being told we were now different people who had different roles to play. And yet we were still just plain old us.

After sitting on the couch together for some time, processing, he wanted to go upstairs to clean his home office and then do sit-ups. *What kind of father has a messy office?* he asked. *What kind of father is out of shape?* He wanted to show you he had his shit together.

I didn't feel the same way. I knew I'd never have my shit together.

During the Renaissance, when a woman discovered she was pregnant with her first child, she'd set about writing a will, so dangerous was the occupation of bringing life into the world.

The idea of death does present itself to me early on, but not my own—yours.

I hold that possibility within my body.

I worry you've died inside me—and I don't know how it would feel to have death inside. There's a phenomenon called a silent miscarriage where an embryo or fetus dies with no external indicators.

I can't stand the idea of not knowing, even for a second.

It's this thought that leads me to rent a device called a doppler, which allows me to listen to your heart. It sends high-frequency waves into my uterus that can detect your heart beating in there. It looks a bit like a trucker's radio. I use it every day to assure myself you are still alive. This is how much I worry.

Your heart goes so fast it sounds like a machine inside my machine.

We decide to tell a few select people about you while it's still early. We call your dad's mother. She asks how far along I am, and we tell her. There's a pause. *Do I have to count the weeks backward,* she says, *to determine if the baby was conceived before or after the wedding?* Your dad asks if she's kidding. She isn't. He responds that it was indeed before. She recovers herself quickly and congratulates us. She's thrilled: her first grandchild. I see it as a brief loss of her usual grace, all her childhood Sundays at Mass taking over.

But what did the date of your conception mean for her— about you, about me—in that split second?

Intellectually, I had always known that cells dividing and organs forming in a woman's body—ones that could become a fetus—make some people feel they have a stake in that body, a say over it, or, like in this case, a right to the details of a woman's sex life. And I had always despised this.

But when I actually experience this relatively minor trespass, I get a very small taste of the deep violation that occurs when the state tries to force a woman to carry a fetus to term through legislation. If you were unwanted, if you came at the wrong time, the panic and horror of it not being anything but my own decision.

I want to know why dividing cells, even a fetus, makes a woman's body public property.

This question of personhood—of if and when these cells, this fetus, has rights—rights that trump those of the woman who grew them, is deeply misogynistic.

I can only see hatred and dehumanization of women underpinning this viewpoint. The argument of anti-abortionists is that life is sacred, yet the idea that the sacredness of life yet lived is more sacred than a living woman's mental and physical well-being is simply an argument against women.

In 2007, for the Turnaway Study, researchers recruited over one thousand women from the waiting rooms of abortion clinics in California, some of whom were denied abortions because they had gone past the gestational limit set by the clinic, and some of whom received the abortions they sought. The women in this study were interviewed twice a year for the next five years regarding numerous measures of physical, psychological, and emotional well-being. In the following years, the women who received the abortions they wanted were more likely to be in romantic relationships they described as "very good," less likely to be experiencing intimate partner violence, were more likely to become intentionally pregnant in the following years, were less likely to be on public assistance, and less likely to report not having enough money for transportation, food, or housing. In addition, if they had other children, those children were also less likely to be living in poverty. They also reported that their physical health was better. While none of the women who received abortions died, two women who were denied the abortions they sought went on to die from pregnancy-related complications.

The life of a woman carrying a fetus is a fully formed one, one in motion, and she should not have to give her life or body over to another if she cannot or does not want to.

Getting to plan for you is a huge privilege.
So was being able to conceive you.
I promise not to forget this.

At twelve weeks gestation, your dad and I go to a concert. We sip water at a table and our feet stick to the floor and nothing is as charming about this venue as we'd previously thought. Our friends do shots of Jameson and clutch one another. We're outcasts in our sobriety.

Back when we were discussing getting pregnant, I had your father agree he'd also stop drinking while I was growing you. It's the least he could do—that's the way I see it. My body is building you cell by cell, leaving me exhausted and sick, while he continues on unencumbered. He sleeps and eats and moves and feels just as he did before. All he's had to do on this journey so far is enjoy an orgasm.

Many of our friends and family members see this arrangement as cruel and totalitarian. I have your father on a tight leash, they say. When I'm not around, they urge him to be reasonable and have a few drinks. *After all*, they tell him, *your wife isn't here, she'll never know.*

A few days later, we go for an ultrasound. We see you.

It's something, I admit it—it gives me the sense you are real—a glimpse of a body inside my body. Before, I thought, *My god, it could be anything in there.*

As the ultrasound technician passes the wand over my belly, you are moving your hands so much it looks like you're waving. Occasionally, you make a jerky movement, like you're doing the electric slide. You refuse to move into a position that would allow the tech to take the measurements she needs and I'm proud of this: *You're a cheeky baby,* I tell your father after, *a rebel.* Of course, I know this is all a projection—my first—and suddenly I'm thinking about projections—the ones mothers make—their damage.

After Ted Bundy was convicted and had even confessed his crimes on tape, his mother Louise exclaimed that her son *does not go around killing women and little children!*

He was the best son in the world, she said.

During this scan, they also check for signs that indicate you may have certain conditions, some of which, as they put it, "are not compatible with life."

After a handful of weeks of holding the idea of your life in my mind, it feels almost impossible to accept that nothing guarantees your survival now or ever. It's a dark, bottomless void hanging under everything—the ultrasound clinic, my bedroom, this city's sidewalks.

I leave the ultrasound room feeling the weight and threat of randomness, which plays a part in each event and choice that leads to the beginning and end of our existences.

Say I didn't meet your father at that party in my friends' basement apartment, my lips stained red with wine, his skinny tie and full lips catching my eye. Or that months later, he hadn't decided to say hello to me at the bottom of the church steps outside of that wedding, or that I didn't take him to bed that night after the reception, then do it again and again.

Say we'd fought and turned away from each other the night you were conceived.

Say the egg had buried itself in my fallopian tube.

And yet the idea of fate, however foolish, is always hovering in my mind.

Your dad and I didn't live in the same city when we started dating, but we couldn't stay away from each other. We frequently drove hundreds of miles for entire weekends inside bedrooms. People in our lives said, *But there are plenty of people here, in this city, down the street, at that bar*, and there were, but we didn't want them. I don't know if that's romance or some biological imperative. Maybe they're the same thing.

It is strange to refer to Clay as your father, especially because I'm still getting used to calling him my husband. I'm dazzled by the way one person can shift through multiple relationships to us: stranger, lover, boyfriend, ex-boyfriend, husband, co-parent. As these shifts happen, I get to see different sides of him, a new person emerging. The same traits reflected at different angles.

As my soon-to-be co-parent, your father's conviction that everything will be all right strikes me as protective and steadying instead of maddeningly naïve as it did when he was my boyfriend, my ex-boyfriend. It's an antidote to my pessimism, though I hadn't previously seen it that way.

Once upon a time, your father was my ex-boyfriend. We broke up for over a year. If it had stuck, you would not be.

An Italian woman once told me relationships are the hardest thing we ever do. I was standing in her kitchen drinking a glass of water and had just asked if she still lived with the father of her daughter. I didn't realize at the time what an incredible gem of wisdom she was offering me.

At some point, your father and I started being very mean to each other. I would drink and say vicious things. He'd break up with me then ask me to take him back a few days later. I'd refuse and disappear for a while. We both had our grievances. We became so mean we decided to split up—we didn't want to be cruel to each other anymore.

We'd come to each other from opposite places. He'd just gone back to university, and I'd already finished two degrees. He was searching for a long-term partner, and I'd just broken up with one. I was faithless and skeptical. He was naïve and disingenuous.

When he turned down a scholarship at his dream school in order to go to a university in a town closer to me, I was too scared to move there with him. I was terrified of following a man and being somewhere without a purpose; I was working in bars and trying to write poetry, making painfully slow progress. He had goals and purpose and was making his way to a "real" career; I was jealous, full of pride. He found me cold and uncaring.

We fought and misbehaved and fought, and when I finally moved to be with him, the damage was too deep.

On our last night together before parting ways, we slept on a mattress on the floor of the attic bedroom in the first house we ever shared together and had feverish sex, the only thing we've ever been consistently good at. I was sure that after the next morning, when we would each unpack our respective belongings from our shared U-Haul, I would never see him again. I knew that if I saw him again, we would get back together, and we were no good together, so I took up an invitation to join friends on a literary tour in Europe. I needed to get far away, and no place seemed farther than bookstores and tiny bars in Edinburgh and Berlin, all glowing with the promise of anonymity. There were no bars or street corners or subway stations there that spoke to me of your father.

My sadness took on a cinematic quality in Europe. I remember biking down what was once the runway at Tempelhof—a former airport in Berlin, now a massive park—considering the moment I would stop thinking about your dad and feeling, foolishly, like there was something grand in my sadness.

That's how much of a kid I was, still am.

Maybe you want to know how we ended up back together. It's not very exciting. I visited a cousin in the city where your father lived and ended up seeing him.

I was dating someone else at the time—and though he did not make my blood rush (nor did I make his), he was brilliant and kind, and I was happy with my life.

I thought I would be safe from whatever pull your dad and I had on each other. And yet I remember hesitating before I booked my train tickets, saying to myself, *This is a bad idea.*

While I was visiting, I got together with two close friends who were also friends with your father, and they invited him to join us.

When I saw him again for the first time, I thought, *This person glows.*

Before he was my boyfriend and then ex-boyfriend, there was a night at a wedding, the second time your dad and I had ever spoken. A bunch of us went back to an apartment we were crashing at to drink some more. Your father came.

I'd gotten a lift to that out-of-town wedding with an acquaintance who was also an old friend of your dad's. In the taxi from the venue to the apartment, she claimed him.

We slept together years ago, she told me, her hand on my arm. *You're not allowed to fuck him.*

I found this claim of proprietorship absurd, and I was voracious then.

As often is the case with relationships, we were so generous to each other in the beginning.

Things deteriorate.
    We let them.

They say people don't change. I know you will hear this in your lifetime. Please, don't believe it, because it is the belief that makes it true. Your father and I changed. We learned to be kind to each other. We learned how rare what we had was and how to take care of it.

We aren't perfect, that's not what I'm saying. But we aren't like before. We don't tear into each other's deepest vulnerabilities. We don't leave.

Before, well, I have to tell you about before because it scares me.

Your father once told me he thought I was the most interesting, intelligent, and beautiful woman he'd ever met, but that it didn't matter because I would always be miserable.

You are *supposed* to feel that first part—that your lover is the most, most, most—but what he was really telling me was that whatever good I had—and he truly believed I had a lot of good, I would only end up ruining it.

It's devastating how the people we love most sometimes choose to provoke our deepest fears.

I had a habit then—one I maintain—of collapsing into periods of hating myself, where I attack the person I am and anyone who tries to defend me. The hatred arrives out of nowhere, making me feel intense disgust for both minute and significant aspects of my being—the size of my pores, my self-consciousness, how I will boast sometimes out of insecurity. I become angry and ashamed and afraid that I don't possess any of the qualities I have been taught make someone worthy, any of the qualities I allow myself to think I have when the specter of that critical voice isn't haunting me. This leads to despair, but instead of allowing myself to feel that despair—which seems unbearable—I get angry.

Anger is easier.

It is a twisted defense mechanism of sorts, born out of a need to protect myself from being vulnerable—any belief others believe in me, like me, or love me needs to be destroyed before another person disabuses me of this notion.

I am circling the idea that hatred comes from fear.

I am afraid.

Maybe I am extraordinarily sensitive and extraordinarily vulnerable.

We all are, but it appears I still don't understand how to cope with this.

These rages would paralyze your father. He detested the part of me that hated myself. Your father is level-headed and self-assured. He doesn't understand self-hatred. He cannot find it in himself to understand how I could have a force inside me so critical of the gentle, loving me, the me he sees as the true Katherine.

Why couldn't I just stop? he wanted to know.

I'm going to find a woman and get married, he said, by which I knew he meant a normal, happy woman—*and we are never, ever going to talk to you.*

Leave, he said, *take everything. I don't want to see even one of your fucking bobby pins.*

It feels urgent to understand this self-hatred, baby, before I become your mother.

Because I remember nights on the floor of apartment bedrooms thinking about hurting myself to relieve the pain. Catching glimpses of my pale face in the mirror and seeing something warped and monstrous—something so cold that I wanted to black it out.

I don't want to pass this poignant self-hatred on to you, like perhaps my father passed it on to me.

My father never fell into self-loathing quite like I do, but he has always chastised himself viciously for small mistakes. And he had great trouble accepting the imperfections in others as well. In his small children, for example. Their fidgeting, their spilling of drinks, their inability to understand certain concepts.

That's all I want to say about that.

I don't blame my father. This was only one side of him.

He warmed the car for my mother every morning in winter and brought her tea. He set out the cereal for us, aligning our spoons neatly beside bowls. He made peanut butter and jam sandwiches for my brother and me every day and packed them in brown bags. He walked us to school and was late to work so he could do all this.

He wanted me to play hockey. He was my baseball coach. There was nothing I could not do because I was a girl, nothing he didn't talk to me about: astrophysics, math, World War II. *Follow your dreams*, he told me, and he meant it.

He was excited about showing me the world. He held my hand and hugged me every night. He was always there to read me a book and take me for a swim at the cottage we rented, show me the stars through his telescope.

Here are our patterns of kindness, waiting to be repeated.
There are our flaws, threatening to be inherited.

I was convinced my body wouldn't be able to make babies. I had the idea I was "barren." I used that particular word—*barren*—said it to myself. It was an insult. It conjures the image of winter in a female body: inhospitable, frigid, bleak sidewalks and biting cold.

That I factored my ability to procreate or lack thereof into my sexuality is odd, considering how divorced sex now is from reproduction.

Women's bodies are expected to hold conflicting desires—the opportunity for casual sex with no threat of pregnancy *and* the possibility of giving someone a baby. It's sexy to look fertile, even though what constitutes looking fertile might be up for debate and is forever shifting. This speaks to the impossible pressures on women: that their bodies must project the idea that they could give men babies—even while bearing most of the responsibility to not get pregnant with those babies.

Our bodies are the backdrop for male fantasy, a fantasy that reminds me of the one anti-abortionists have, one that relies on the notion our bodies are part of their narrative, not our own.

If a woman's body cannot make children, she is perhaps all the lusher and more fertile—for her own pleasure, for self-exploration, for making use of her body for herself only, or for her lovers. She gives fruit to so much else.

Why didn't I let myself see my own body that way when I thought I could not have children? By using misogyny against myself in this way, I used it against all women.

I don't want to deny here the heartbreak of infertility for wom-en who would like to conceive children—I have read and lis-tened to women discuss the profound grief of this experience, and I can imagine. There needs to be much more space for those discussions.

But I do want to deny the narrative of the barren body. A fe-male body, alive and experiencing the world, is always enough.

I was also just not sure I wanted children. I never felt that keenness some women have told me they feel when they see babies. I am extremely uncomfortable with the fragility of newborns, the dawdling and repetition of children, their sticky fingers. I have no patience. I thought I may only want to be a visitor in their lives.

And yet the experience of it is so compelling. Compulsion is a selfish reason for having a child, but all the reasons are—I don't see any justification for it.

I am not sure I could give you a satisfying answer as to why I finally decided I did want kids.

There's the fact that I have always liked playing with children. They are fun, free, wild, and creative. They are honest, which I appreciate. I grew up with a lot of little cousins. I babysat kids in my neighborhood. Caring for them could be monotonous, yes, but there were also glimpses of joy and intimacy that pulled at me. I understood I could appreciate and have relationships with kids without raising my own, but I wondered about the intimacy between a mother and her child, how that would be.

I also recognize that society has impressed upon me that motherhood is the natural and most fulfilling role for women to take on. I detest this—and I have tried to separate my own feelings about the choice from that inherited idea, but that can feel like such an impossible challenge—untangling what your true feelings are and where they've come from. Like trying to erase my desire to be thin, I have adopted certain feelings I can never fully escape. But what is society's promise of motherhood? Fulfillment? Fulfillment of what? Some of my friends have spoken about a biological tug, like the animal in them demanded a baby. Is it the fulfilling of that tug, some innate desire to continue our species? Or of a duty, to do what our parents did, to carry on the family tree? To carry on humanity. (It would be very easy to argue humanity should not be carried on.)

A more cynical view might be that it is the ultimate fulfillment of the role set out for my gender: relentless caregiving, loving, cooking, cleaning. Unending sacrifice and selflessness.

But I think when it comes down to it, I saw motherhood as one of life's more intense, all-consuming experiences—and I am attracted to those.

I find this question as hard to answer as *Why did you want to fall in love?*

Motherhood is its own falling in love, and I have always loved being in love.

We all had mothers, every single one of us. This might not seem like a revelation, but when I got pregnant, it was—the fact that so many other women had gone through this experience that felt so singular.

I wasn't special at all.

SECOND TRIMESTER

Autumn

The experience of pregnancy essentializes. A woman with the body of a pregnant woman tells her story often, and re-tells it, to the people who are close to her and to strangers.

—Anna Prushinskaya, *A Woman Is a Woman Until She Is a Mother*

I'm encouraged to tell people about you now because we've passed the threshold of the first trimester, which carries the most significant risk of miscarriage. I find myself still wanting to keep you a secret, though, because I like my privacy. Announcing my pregnancy feels like handing myself over to the public for scrutiny.

How far along are you?

Boy or girl?

First time?

How do you feel?

I hide my growing belly under long sweaters as the air turns crisp.

Last summer I accompanied my cousin and her two small children to a small suburban beach in the middle of the week. I had imagined we'd be the only people there, but as the day wore on, the beach quickly filled up with mothers, children, umbrellas, sunscreen bottles, and sand buckets.

There wasn't a man in sight.

I felt tight. I didn't want to meet other mothers or their wet, sandy children because I didn't want to start chatting about ice cream and bedtime, which is what I'd observed mothers talking to each other about, and which is what we ended up doing for part of our outing. I had wanted to talk about my struggle to find a job or what my cousin was reading or how we were currently feeling about our own mothers.

While I was curious about the larger aspects of motherhood—how it felt to love so profoundly, for example, or the experience of labor—I felt scornful of the small stuff, like tantrums and toilet training, though only when a stranger attempted to talk to me about it. I didn't mind chatting with my cousin about it. Maybe my attitude doesn't sound too unfair, but I would never feel such contempt if I had to discuss menial aspects of other work or topics outside of my own experience with strangers. Boredom, maybe, but not the irritation I felt when I heard about the drudge of mothering. The practical and repetitive tasks that inform motherhood—changing diapers, giving baths, organizing playdates—are not given any status or respect by the outside world, so talking about them with a woman I knew only as a mother grated on me. I think it made me feel as if she was reinforcing the sexist stereotype that women lose themselves in motherhood (whatever losing oneself means in this context), that motherhood can be like a pair of blinders on a horse, preventing a woman from seeing anything beyond loving and caring for her child. I know this stereotype is just that—being very invested in your child does not mean you can't be invested in other things, but it's also that the actual work of raising children is shunned. Society attaches so much value to the concept of the mother—lifting her up as an abstract—while also denigrating and devaluing her work. Although the *idea* of the mother might be glorified, the day-to-day of her life certainly is not, so we don't want to actually look at—or listen—to her.

☽

I have in my mind this image of a mother with her tote bag full of diapers and snacks, frazzled—a baby on her hip and a strap falling down her shoulder.

It is the opposite of glamour. Every aspirational image of a woman that is sold to me is one of glamour. The woman in the handbag advertisement strides across a New York street, her spotless cashmere coat catching the breeze, every hair in place.

Mothers clean and care for other bodies and get messy doing it. This does not merit looking.

There is something in not being looked at—a freedom.

Although, that's also privileged nonsense. Everyone deserves to be seen. And I recognize there is a long history of women not being seen because their bodies don't resemble the white, thin, young, able-bodied ideal sketched out by our racist, ableist, ageist, fat-phobic society. I recognize my white, able body gives me a specific type of visibility that protects me from certain forms of discrimination, violence, dehumanization, and surveillance and I've often taken the comfort and privileges this allows me for granted.

But what I mean by not being looked at is not being looked at by men in that hungry way, not being subject to the male gaze, like that woman in the advertisement.

☽

Young women are looked at in that hungry way a lot, baby. This trains women to watch themselves from the outside, like the men and the women who have adopted the male gaze do. It's like having an out-of-body experience.

I found this effect uncomfortable, damaging even. The gaze itself occasionally made me feel important or special, though in reality, the reasons I was being looked at—my youth and my femaleness—did not make me special at all.

I was self-conscious of this looking and whether I fit the role being looked at suggested I was supposed to play. I spent far too much mental energy thinking about whether I was attractive enough, thin enough, to be looked at. Was I good enough for the attention I hadn't even asked for?

That energy should have gone elsewhere. Thinking about that looking is distracting.

And so, here I am finding the idea of a certain invisibility appealing, like it might make me better by allowing me to harness that brainpower toward pursuits and ideas I find more interesting.

I tell work about you. I'm a scriptwriter and researcher at a local production company that makes food television.

My boss loves to talk about pregnancy and veers our meetings in that direction. He tells me how his first wife became a different person after she left her job and became a stay-at-home mother. He says she started drinking white wine in the afternoons and talking obsessively about happenings in the neighborhood.

I think about how the business of stay-at-home moms is making connections—building a network to maintain your sanity and help grow your child, so talking about neighbors seems important and strategic.

I don't say this out loud because my boss doesn't like to be contradicted.

My boss now has a second, younger wife and a new baby. He refers to her as his "supermodel wife" and says his first wife is jealous and always attempting to spite him.

I wonder why he thinks it is okay to talk to me this way—I'm a pregnant thirty-something woman who has the capacity to relate to and empathize with other women. Does he believe I take solace in not being "that type" of woman, in drawing a line between his ex and myself? What type of woman am I?

I smile up at him from my chair on the other side of his desk. I'm a coward.

☽

I have had so many conversations like this with men in my lifetime, in which they expect me to accept and hold on to negative statements about other women. I think men know women of my generation have been taught to compete with each other and they take advantage of that weakness, the implication being if they're including us in the conversation, we're different—we're not like other women.

You're not like other women, he said, he said, he said.

I want to be like other women. I think other women are incredible. I want to share them with you once you're out in this world.

I have been silent in these conversations too many times.

I work with some young women who don't stay silent; I watch them and try to learn.

My boss also says he'd like to be able to experience pregnancy and labor himself. He says women are lucky to have these experiences. He says he told his wife all this while she was in labor.

It's jarring to realize how separate men remain from this business of growing children. I know this should have been self-evident, and in some ways, it was, but I thought there'd be some sort of compensating task they did, the men.

As if buying ice cream and rubbing feet could compete with the work I'm doing.

How could there be any equity when I am growing you in my body and your father is not?

When I refer to you while talking to him, I always say *my baby*. Not to be cruel. Not on purpose. It's automatic. How yet are you his? I don't see a connection.

I tell your father all this and he accepts it good-naturedly. He knows very well this is happening in my body.

And yet—beyond the physical—the connection that exists between you and me also seems somewhat tenuous. I don't know you. I often can't even believe you're actually in there. It still seems like such a preposterous thing to believe of my body.

Who are you, baby?

What, even, is your sex?

My friend Kate says she is less curious about which sex her baby is than who her baby is. I get that, and I also aspire to feel that way, but the reality is that I often wonder if you are a boy or a girl.

Knowing your sex would help make you more real to me. It would give me a detail to hang on to. You'd become an outline. I don't accept that if you are a girl, it means *a*, or if you are a boy, it means *b*, but it does mean many people will treat you as if it does, which in turn means I will need to fight against one set of harmful ideas or another for the sake of your happiness, and your goodness.

I read a study that says mothers speak more to their infant daughters than their infant sons, responding more to the vocalizations female infants make. Anne Fausto-Sterling, a leading expert on biology and gender development, reflected on the possible implications of the study in a 2014 *Reuters* article.

> At least within the standard psychological literature there has been a longstanding view that girls develop language skills more quickly than boys. Some researchers believe the difference in language development is innate, but this study suggests that adults may treat infant girls differently than infant boys at a very young age, which may help explain the difference.

I don't know what the researchers behind this thought, but I wonder if the mothers in the study subconsciously assumed daughters were better confidantes. Does it feel more natural to chat with a girl, even if she's still an infant?

No matter your sex, I want to raise you to be an empathetic human who does not intentionally harm others.

It seems so daunting.

I meet a woman wearing fatigues in a restroom. She's a member of the armed forces and she's six months pregnant. She tells me she and her partner did a gender reveal via a cake they had baked for them, pink Smarties spilling out when they sliced into it.

Kathryn Bond Stockton, author of *Gender(s)*, describes the announcement of a baby's gender at a birth functioning like a "cone pulled down on the body."

With the advent of regular ultrasounds, that cone comes down much earlier.

"Only later will the word get *inside the child* to become a word that stands for the child itself (if the child will stand for it)," she writes.

> Even more dramatically, the child's sex word, pronounced at birth, is a gender-word: "it's a girl!" or "it's a boy!" The idiom is not "it's a male!" or "it's a female!" An entire world of cultural assumptions is rolled up into the word rolled on the baby and its genitals.

In our so-called "gender" reveals, pink Smarties or blue balloons or the simple announcement from the ultrasound tech covers the baby in meaning while it's still in a person's uterus, dictates how we think of it, plan to dress it or treat it, or the dreams we have for it. I don't want to confine you within these norms, but I am so eager to connect with you, and these ideas about sex and gender, no matter how forced or false, provide me with a shape to grasp on to.

Motherlike

My mother says lots of parents focus on their children becoming smart and successful, handsome or beautiful, but what she wanted most was for her kids to be kind and happy.

Kind and happy.

That seems like an impossible proposition for most people these days.

My mother is the kindest person I know.

She is fiercely intelligent, though her warmth—her kind openness—is the more visible element of her being. People want to tell her things, even people who don't know her.

For decades she taught Special Education in the Toronto District School Board, caring about every student profoundly, referring to her students as "my kids," and talking about them so fondly that people thought she was talking about her biological children.

Ever since I was little, she let me have big parties, but the rule was that I had to invite every single person in my class. Leaving someone out was not an option. We had a Halloween party where every single person got to carve their own pumpkin. We had a party for my springtime birthday where she agreed to play the Disney video for "Monster Mash" on repeat in the family room, while the kids ran around outside and inside through our patio door. She made box cakes and bought premade frosting. When we went grocery shopping, I got to pick out whatever I wanted, within reason.

When I got upset, she wrapped me in her long arms, told me everything was going to be okay, and that I could do whatever would make me feel better.

She didn't like to tell me "no," though she did when she had to. She believed in fun. I want to be like this as a mother.

Baby, her voice on the telephone—it's like the sun and the sand and the waves flooding through the speaker.

No matter who you are, baby, she has so much love for you.

But, sweet babe, my mother—your grandmother—still lives in Toronto.

We don't.

Why have I done that? Who will I hand you over to on the days when I can't do it anymore?

That human females live beyond their reproductive age is unique; the only other animals who live decades past their ability to reproduce are short-finned pilot whales and killer whales.

In the sixties, evolutionary biologists came up with a theory to explain this. "The Grandmother Theory" posits that a grandmother's usefulness in helping her offspring raise and support her grandchildren was responsible for this adaptation of living beyond reproduction. If a grandmother can help forage for food for her grandbabies, or hold the baby while mom forages, that family is going to benefit, and those babies are going to have the longevity gene their grandmother did.

Some subsequent research has supported this hypothesis. From tracing birth and death records of families in seventeenth- and eighteenth-century Quebec and eighteenth- and nineteenth-century Finland, researchers discovered that women who lived close to their mothers (i.e., in the same parish) not only had more children and started having children younger, but also that the mortality rate of children aged two to five dropped significantly (though only if the grandmother was under seventy-five years of age).

Whatever knowledge or resources those mamas' mamas had to give was particularly helpful in keeping children aged two to five years old alive.

Many new mothers I know don't let their mothers mother their children. They take their advice sparingly, turning to the medical establishment and current parenting theories instead. I doubt I will be any different.

In her book, *Women as Mothers*, social anthropologist Sheila Kitzinger writes:

> In our own society grandmothers are above all ex-mothers. They are people who have finished doing a task. They may be allowed to have a hand in mothering, and be permitted to re-enact their own mother experience spasmodically and in a modified way with their grandchildren, but they in effect "play" at mothering only on occasion when this is agreed by the real mother, or in situations of crisis when their help is sought because of the inability to cope or absence of the real mother.

And later: "The grandmother's overtures to the grandchild may be accepted with varying degrees of tolerance."

My instinct here is to attribute this change to scientific progress. We know, for example, that putting babies to sleep on their backs reduces the rate of SIDS significantly, where my mother's generation was told it was safer to put a baby down to sleep on her belly. We wouldn't listen to our mothers on this topic, though that assumes she would not accept new data-proven information about children's safety.

What about the rest of a grandmother's knowledge? I can see how a trend of not letting our mothers mother denies and disrespects their knowledge.

I have the urge to mother in my own way. I don't know if this is simply a desire to establish my own way of being a mother, to separate myself—as the daughter—from my mother, or if trusting other parenting experts over my own mother is a result of internalized misogyny. I turn to books for advice, books written by experts, but most advice has not been "proven" as more effective than other methods. Sleep training versus no sleep training. Gentle parenting versus parenting with stricter methods. As far as I can tell, it is all still contested.

Why then, do I turn to it more instead of asking my mother?

I know so many women with difficult, even toxic relationships with their mothers.

How does this play out when a baby arrives?

I'm getting nervous.

In the years leading up to this pregnancy, I told your father all the horrible things I'd ever heard about having children, in the same way I told him all the horrible things I'd ever heard about getting married before we got married. I did this because he's idealistic and idealism frightens me. I wanted him to know how tough it was going to be so he wouldn't feel trapped, even though he always wanted marriage and children more than I did.

I don't like the idea of having anything to do with trapping men, even though, despite the stereotype of women trapping men with children and marriage, it is men who have been trapping women for centuries, both systematically and individually. What men mean when they say women "trap" them is that sometimes women—and the communities that support them—insist they act like decent, responsible human beings and live with the consequences of their actions. Insist they parent, too.

Men can trap women in a tangible, physical way.

Your dad tells me it has been a dream of his since he was little to be "trapped" by a family. He has always wanted a house, a marriage, and children. He wants to be able to create a happy home and his own family dynamics.

When I met your dad, he played guitar in a very loud rock band, had a partially shaved head, had a reputation for being popular with women. His suburban dreams still surprise me.

He hates when I talk about being trapped—that I associate you with that. He wants me to know it is my choice—and if I choose it, then it's not a trap.

I always felt trapped in the "Katherine" I had become—or was expected to be (I'm not sure I could tell the difference between the two), so I always adored an escape hatch. I've spent a lot of time running from my life. Running to other countries, convinced I could escape myself and become a different person by being far from home. I couldn't.

And I can't run from you. Or rather, I don't want to. And for a while, you won't be able to run from me either.

Running is one of the ways women survive misogyny. Every woman finds a different way.

I tried running, but my favorite survival mechanism was building a misogynist in my brain—he is at the heart of that ever-present critical voice I wrote to you about before. He complicates my self-hatred. He's vicious. But I keep him there so he can tell me all the hurtful things the world thinks about me—me as a woman—before the world tells me. Again, this comes down to protecting an excruciating vulnerability.

The trouble now is you—you adopting or internalizing that voice.

This is the danger. Or this is the whole game of reproduction. *What are we reproducing?* is a question I should have asked myself.

I'm not the only woman with a misogynist living inside. Some women don't even realize he's there.

☽

Donald Trump wins the American presidency.

My belly is a swollen hill.

As I ride the bus to work the morning after the news, I think about the type of world I am bringing you into—where the leader of the most powerful nation in the world is a man accused of raping his ex-wife, a man who boasted about grabbing women's vulvas and getting away with it, a man who has publicly referred to women as "fat pigs."

Poll figures vary, but it seems at least forty-seven per cent of white women in the United States voted for Trump, which is evidence of internalized misogyny. Women can have valid reasons for not voting for Hillary Clinton, his opponent, but choosing a man who openly insults, objectifies, and demeans women can only be explained by the fact that those women believe it is okay to treat women that way. And *that*—just like my scorn for the work of mothers—is internalized misogyny.

Certain days I write to you as the day gets dark and the street-lights come on.

I beg you to make it out safely into this world, despite everything unkind in it.

There is a long list of things pregnant women are told not to do. And when I say told, I mean it.

As economist and author Emily Oster points out in her book *Expecting Better*, when a pregnant woman goes to the doctor, she is not informed about the data we have about the risks of certain behaviors while pregnant and then left to make up her own mind. She is simply told what not to do, even when the information we have does not back up such decrees. For example, the current data we have on consuming an occasional glass of alcohol while pregnant does not indicate any harm to the fetus, though it has also not ruled it out. Women are told to avoid all alcohol consumption based on information we have about children of mothers who drank more heavily, meaning at least daily, or who participated in binge drinking (which is always dangerous during pregnancy). Indeed, in an analysis of studies involving 150,000 pregnancies that sought to link low-level alcohol consumption and abnormal pregnancy outcomes, researchers were unable to show a statistically significant link.

I'm not arguing that pregnant women should drink (indeed, alcohol has now definitively been proven to be bad for you, pregnant or not pregnant), but I do think doctors should make the lack of evidence clear and let women make up their own minds, just as they should with all the other risks, such as eating deli meats. What is the exact risk I will hurt you, baby, if I have a slice of salami one afternoon? Pregnant women are told not to eat deli meats because they can carry the bacteria listeria, which could cause listeriosis and seriously harm or kill a fetus. But listeria can also live on cantaloupe and mushrooms and stone fruits.

This paucity of information from the doctor about the risks of behaviors when it comes to reproduction is part of a larger pattern. I was not adequately informed of the risks oral birth control could pose to my physical or mental well-being when I asked for a prescription, as if the doctor was happy to overlook it for the sake of ensuring I didn't get pregnant, while, when it comes to the life inside my body, I am not given choices but absolutes, as if—once again—I do not deserve to make my own choices about my own body.

Another activity I am told not to do is drink coffee, my lifeblood. That's right, I'm more tired than I've ever been in my entire life, but I am supposed to cut most of my caffeine intake and continue on. Less than 200 milligrams per day is safe, according to most studies, but then a new study will pop up that says, well, maybe any amount of caffeine leads to lower birth weights, but it's just one study that contradicts many others that found a cup has no effect, and I'm left feeling mad trying to navigate all this.

Another thing I'm not supposed to do is stress. Stress can apparently lead to preterm birth and low birth weight. Of all the *do nots*, I have not figured this one out. And I feel stressed over the suggestion I may be hurting you by being stressed. I'm expected to work and retain all of my normal responsibilities, so I don't understand this expectation that I can suddenly eliminate all my stress.

Some stress is okay, I once read on a website for expectant mothers.

How much is *some*?

What if I'm the type of person who seeks out stress like a sport?

Lately, I've been worrying incessantly about that adolescent moment when you decide to open your laptop and find porn. Porn like the porn I've seen on the internet, where many of the women enjoy or pretend to enjoy humiliation. The male bodies are imperfect and violent, and the female bodies are flawless and gagging and bending. I know there are deviations from this formula, but this is the predominant one. I'm not anti-porn, but I worry about mainstream porn being your primary means of instruction.

If you identify as male and like women, how will these images affect you? What will you expect of girls? What will turn you on? What will you ask them to do?

And if you identify as female and like men, how will these images affect you? What will the boys you date expect of you? What will you expect of yourself? What will you like?

And if you are attracted to your own gender, I'd have a lot to learn because I am not well-versed in queer pornography.

From talking to other expectant mothers, it does not seem standard to think about this when you are a nineteen-week-old fetus.

When I talk about stress, I become aware of my privilege. My concerns seem trivial. I feel silly and oblivious.

I read in the *New York Times* that Black mothers in the US are more likely to have babies who are preterm and underweight—and researchers believe it may be due to the accumulated stress from experiencing racism and sexism every single day (this, and the wearing down of the body it causes, is referred to as "allostatic load"). Black women are also three to four times more likely to die from childbirth or pregnancy-related causes than white women in America and are more likely to report discrimination and mistreatment during medical care. (In Canada, we unfortunately don't collect data on this, so I can't speak to the statistics here.)

In an investigation undertaken by journalists Nina Martin and Renee Montagne for ProPublica entitled "Nothing Protects Black Women From Dying in Pregnancy and Childbirth," ProPublica and NPR collected hundreds of stories from Black mothers in the US and found that the "feeling of being devalued and disrespected by medical providers was a constant theme" and that "doctors and nurses didn't take their pain seriously."

Countless studies in North America and the UK back this up: doctors consistently underestimate the pain their Black patients are in, which, during pregnancy and childbirth, has devastating consequences.

I see many images of fetuses in the womb while I'm pregnant with you, baby, but I won't see a detailed anatomical picture of a

Black woman carrying a fetus until years after your birth, while I'm editing this book, and Nigerian medical student Chidiebere Ibe illustrates one that goes viral on social media.

In North America, motherhood is still predominantly represented as white. Many Black scholars, writers, and celebrities have spoken about this invisibility (as well as hypervisibility in certain spaces), both within the framework of pregnancy and in general.

In an interview with the *Guardian*, writer Claudia Rankine once stated, "the invisibility of Black women is astounding."

As I move through pregnancy as a white woman, I think of my visibility and all that entails. I take for granted representations of myself—or medical care without discrimination—that I don't suffer the added stress of racism, that I'm seen.

And I want to tell you about it, baby, not as an exercise of confession, but an impetus to action, as an ongoing look at being a white mother and how I contribute to systems of oppression.

I am putting another white kid in this world. I better be fucking responsible.

I read that your experiences in the womb will shape your brain and play a part in who you are. I am horrified by this idea. I am emotionally and situationally irresponsible with myself—it is my right to be. I let myself travel to the most extreme limit of my emotions. I approach the most devastating books, movies, and art with open arms, no matter how fragile I might be feeling, willing myself to be devastated. I embrace confrontations and situations I know are potentially explosive.

I hadn't realized the extent to which you are along for the ride.

Growing up, one way I'd observed women operating in the world—my mother being one of them—was to exist in a general mode of happiness and denial, not looking too hard at things in case they were too hard to look at. Like daughters sometimes do, I insisted on the opposite: I was going to examine and interrogate everything. I didn't want to be numb to anything—I wanted to make sure I was here for it.

But most of the time, *it* is too much.

My mother has a rule that she will not cry in front of her children, no matter what. She wants to be a rock for us.

She told me about this rule as we cleaned items out of her mother's house after she died. I sobbed as I worked, my parents silently moving through afghans and oil paintings.

Why aren't you crying? I finally demanded, feeling like an outlier.

My mother is well-intentioned with this, baby—she wants to be the rock for us, and I get that, but I want you to know just how strong and resilient it makes you to be able to express your emotions.

My mother's father was an alcoholic. My mother's father was a wonderful person.

I feel guilty writing that first statement because it tells only one story and seems to cancel out the second.

Somewhere along the way, saying someone was an alcoholic became akin to saying they were defective. This is not true.

Alcohol isn't good for a family, even if my grandfather's alcoholism was the run-of-the-mill variety of his generation of men.

Leaving your kids in the car while you had a drink at the bar was not out of the ordinary in the fifties and sixties.

My mother could not admit her dad's alcoholism to herself until she sat through a session with my therapist at the age of sixty-three and was forced to confront it.

Later, she told me, after sitting with this revelation for a while, her childhood made much more sense to her.

My mother tells me how her mother always worried her father was going to die in a car accident after a night out drinking.

He did, except that's not the full story. The full story is he only had one or two drinks that night, and the accident was essentially unavoidable. On his way home, there was a tow truck parked on the wrong side of the road right after the blind curve of a bend. It had been called to help with an earlier accident. My grandfather swerved to avoid the truck and the people standing outside of it, flipping into a ditch and breaking his neck in the process.

My mother thought and thought about those seconds when his car was hurtling off the road and he knew death was coming. How terrified he must have been.

In my twenties, I dreamed of the accident once, dreamed his face through the windshield, bright lights, and an overturned car, and then him milking cows in a field, peaceful. *Tell her I'm sorry*, he told me.

I wrote my mother an email about the dream the next morning. She never responded.

I was four when he died. I remember the phone call. I remember the funeral, but only the wooden floors and chairs and how his face looked far too smooth.

How do you tell a child about death?

How will I tell you about death when it enters our lives?

There are blankets and blankets of snow in this city; I like how it makes everything quiet.

Can you hear, baby, how the snow makes everything quiet?

When I ask my mother about aging, expecting that she, like so many other women, might be bothered by it, she only comments that perhaps she should have enjoyed her body more at age twenty-five.

But she isn't going to think about it too much, or stare at the back of her thighs in the mirror, like I do. I love this about my mother, but I can't relate.

Thoughts about my body consume me; it annoys the hell out of me. Women who have been through pregnancy go out of their way to tell me my belly will never be flat again, my breasts will look different forever, I'll have stretch marks. I tell myself it should not matter, but I think and think and think about it.

I squint my eyes in the mirror like I'm looking for evidence of the slow destruction of the body I had, as if it were not allowed to change, had not changed a million times already, had not lost and gained fat and muscle, had not dimpled and drooped, sprouted stretch marks and rough patches.

I glare at it as if it is betraying someone.

But not you.

The story of becoming conscious of my body is the story of realizing it wasn't good enough.

When I was six years old, I suddenly decided I needed blonde hair.

I followed my mother around asking her to let me dye it. I have a memory of pestering her about it in the laundry room. She finally gave in and said that while she would not let me dye it, she'd buy me a blonde wig if I was really that desperate.

I considered it, but I knew that wasn't good enough. It wasn't real enough. I'd never be a true blonde like Barbie or Sleeping Beauty.

Already, at six, my body wasn't something I could just exist in. I wanted to alter is so I could be as loved as those fair-haired beauties. I think about how my BIPOC peers must have felt then—how little the media shone a light on their brilliant beauty in that late-eighties/early-nineties timeframe. How ridiculously easy I had it.

☽

Also, at this age, my dad tells me I used to run down the block yelling, *I'm a fast girl!* Joyful in my speed, the wind. Wearing a pair of pale-yellow biker shorts I insisted on putting on every day.

I met that girl again once after I recovered from a spontaneous pneumothorax (a collapsed lung) at nineteen. Bed-bound for weeks, when I was finally able to go for my first jog outside— the joy, the wind, my brilliant working body.

How to hold on to this.

I can remember the feeling of all the bodies I've ever had. The child body. The adolescent body. The early teen body, which suffered from anorexia and stopped menstruating. The young adult body weighed down by excessive drinking in university. The body that lived in Italy, indulged in pasta and pizza and cornetti and came back to Canada fuller. A body crossing the threshold of thirty. This pregnant body, expanding with you.

All these bodies existing in one body.

When I was twenty-nine, I lived in an apartment in a very trendy area of Toronto. In the summertime, my building's lobby door exited right out onto the patio of a popular brunch restaurant. One July morning, after a long shift bartending the previous night, I awoke to an empty fridge and decided to go to the Portuguese bakery a few blocks away for an espresso and a tart. It was stifling hot in my tiny bedroom, so I threw on a tank top and a pair of cut-off jeans. I caught a glance of myself in the mirror and hesitated—the shorts, which I'd cut from an old pair of jeans myself—were really short. If I went out in them, I'd get a lot of attention from men. I didn't want attention. I just wanted food and caffeine. I started to change but then got irritated with myself: If I changed, I was saying I was weak, that I couldn't handle men yelling and looking, that I couldn't just feel free and wear whatever I wanted. I was being incredibly self-absorbed, being so dramatic.

I buttoned the shorts back up.

Then I hesitated again—was I wearing these because some small part of me wanted attention? I really didn't think so, and if I was, so what?

Fuck this! I thought. This should not take so much energy. I'm not doing this.

I grabbed some cash and ran out the door and down the stairs. When I crossed the first busy intersection on that sunny day, two men yelled and whistled at me loudly. Others turned to look. I stiffened, feeling highly self-conscious, but I pretended I was as unaffected as all the other women seemed to be when they got whistled at. I bit my cheek and ducked into the bakery, flushed.

When I was fourteen, I started modelling a little. People kept approaching me about it in shopping malls and on the street. I wasn't particularly interested, but I was also raised at a time when being a model seemed to be the highest accomplishment a woman could achieve, even if my parents themselves hadn't raised me with that message.

A high-end agency sent me to do a photo shoot with a photographer. I didn't know what to do in front of the camera.

Look at the camera like you want to fuck the photographer, said the male makeup artist. And he kept saying it, even though I didn't know how to do that. I'd barely made out with someone, let alone fucked.

In the photos, I look like I'm going to be sick.

After the shoot, the makeup artist told me, *Your hips are always going to be a problem. You could consider a nose job. Change your pillowcase every night so your skin is better.*

Once, one of my agents saw me eating a lollipop while I was crossing the street after a casting near their offices. She phoned me to discuss it, then put me on a diet. I pretended I was consuming what she was telling me to (salads and lemon water mostly), which she also asked me to track and report back about. Instead, I smoked weed and ate candy, drank peach schnapps, and followed my friends to McDonald's.

❧

At that first photo shoot, the clothes they dressed me in were held together on the back side of my body with three huge metal clamps—those industrial ones usually used to hold wire.

It's because they were women's clothes, and I was fourteen. It only occurred to me much later how strange it was that they were using a child as a representation of some sort of ideal woman.

I was such a bad model, in every single way. I was common. I failed all the girls, baby.

I internalized then how my body was not good enough for consumption in those places.

Years later, as a young adult working in bars serving rich men, living in Rome, studying in Montreal, I met a lot of men who admired the bodies of young women, including mine. Restaurants are a place where lots of men consume female bodies, as if they're part of the menu.

Men in those spaces said things that made me nauseous. They said they would leave their wives. They said they couldn't help it. They said they would pay money for it.

Forty-year-old men scoffed to me about forty-year-old women wanting to sleep with them. *Imagine!* they said.

And these men who thought they were flattering me by denigrating older women, saying they'd throw aside their loves for me, only planted me more firmly in my conviction I should never let myself enjoy or trust my body or my youth. *What were they for exactly?*

I would be old, too. I would be the thrown-over. I hated the idea of having to grieve for this because—what was I grieving for exactly—a temporary power afforded to me? But what is that power—the ability to turn certain men on?

We have organized our value system around male lust. Even if the absurdity of this is easy to see, working to escape it still feels like the challenge of my lifetime.

And here I am—mid-thirties and angry at this body, as if it hasn't done so much for me, as if I haven't learned anything.

As if all this time fighting the beliefs that appall me has amounted to nothing.

I just want to learn how to let this body be.

I'm not a service.

A member of your dad's family—a young woman—tells me that her male co-workers have confided in her that having sex with their wives after children isn't the same: their bodies aren't the same—particularly their vaginas. She appears to feel empathy for these men.

❃

Your dad's dad tells me that after his wife's three labors he asked the doctor to put an extra stitch in there for him.

He's not the only one. There's a term for this—the husband stitch.

❃

All this stuff about being tight. The vagina is a muscle. It stretches during labor then retracts again.

❃

I read that porn actresses too old to be in the teen category and too young to be considered MILFs have trouble finding work.

❃

Our bodies are astonishing; these categories reducing.

You grow and grow in me. My body adjusts.

Your dad's father never once expressed concern about my safety before you. Now he hounds your dad to buy us a better car to keep "us" safe. Maybe I'm being cynical, but I believe he is only interested in my safety so that my body can continue to carry you to term.

My body is the vessel.

The thing about this vessel now is how foreign it seems. Last night, I caught a glimpse of it in the bathroom mirror and I thought, *Who is that pregnant woman getting into the shower?*

Earlier in my pregnancy, I looked at my reflection after undressing and found it all somewhat familiar. But now you have stretched my belly so much the skin looks taut to the point of breaking; I can see you moving under it. My reflection is alien.

It is harder to forget about your presence at this point, like I used to, but even the other evening, in a stupor of delirium and energy, I leapt onto the bed belly-first, momentarily forgetting that you existed. I felt sharp pain upon landing and worried I'd hurt you.

☽

I'm sorry, baby. Already I make mistakes.

Those two lines indicating your existence.

At twenty weeks, we are sent for another ultrasound and find out you are a boy. The technician can see your penis right there on the ultrasound.

There it is, she says, gesturing to the screen. I see nothing identifiable.

I'm going to be honest and tell you I wanted a girl. I wanted to raise a strong, confident girl who would become a proud feminist woman. I worry about raising a boy because I think about the harm men do and I worry about contributing to that. I'll raise you as a feminist, but there are so many elements beyond my control, so many outside influences.

I watch a group of preteen boys gathered together near a car one afternoon soon after. They're loud, swaggering, looking at something on one of their phones.

I try not to imagine what's on that phone.

I try to find you in there.

In his book, *Getting Off: Pornography and the End of Masculinity*, Robert Jensen describes his first experience objectifying women as a moment in early grade school when one of his friends found a porn magazine and he and a group of boys crowded around it to look. The nude woman as an image on the page, the boys encircling her, looming above.

Right before Christmas, we tell our family and friends the news you are a boy. On the twenty-fifth, we open the gifts we've received for you: tiny blue socks with miniature footballs on them, a book about a construction site, and a teddy bear wearing a blue handkerchief. As I watch these things accumulate, it becomes more and more strange to me that anyone feels confident saying that boys inherently like trucks and girls inherently love dolls. Both sexes are pushed into a mound of gendered clothing and toys and expectations.

My own mind is an extremely gendered place.

Your dad's family has a lot of men—men who were once boys.

Another boy! everyone says, but it sounds like they're saying *yuck!*

Maybe we shouldn't allow these boys to become so goddamn disgusting.

I dream you are born, and I forget to breastfeed you for weeks. You don't ask, and every time I come home, I intend to, but I never get around to it. It seems so like me. I've never even kept a plant alive.

Each morning I teeter with the weight of you to work over the ice, through the park across from the river, the profound cold making the old snow crisp and sharp. The path I take is not really a path but a place I have trodden down. When I see the sun, I feel almost happy, like I've arrived somewhere.

THIRD TRIMESTER

Winter

Pregnancy is hell.

—Cashier at a baby store in my neighborhood

Pregnancy turns the body grotesque: huge tits, areolae, and belly. Everything swollen.

Today I find it disgusting and perverse, can't locate any beauty in it.

❋

During pregnancy, women's areolae will darken and enlarge, our uteruses stretch to many times their original size, our joints and ligaments loosen, our blood volume doubles.

In this final trimester, our ribs flare out and expand in response to the uterus, which is now large enough to push right up beneath the rib cage. You're in there growing and kicking up at my newly expanded ribs.

At this point I'm so tired with work and life and hosting you that my brain invents things. The other night I thought men were shining flashlights through our bedroom windows, but it was just a car pulling into the driveway of the house behind ours.

Tick, tick, tick—my body just keeps making you. My brain can't catch up.

One of my grandmothers worked at a famous advertising agency in Toronto before she got pregnant with my father.

She quit when she got pregnant.

Why? I asked.

That's just how it was—she said. *They didn't want pregnant women at work.*

✳

A woman with the body of a pregnant woman tells her story often, and retells it, to the people who are close to her and to strangers.

My mother was pregnant with me is a thought I keep having.
    This is strange information.

❄

When I was very small, I never wanted to be without my mother.
    I've never seen such devotion in a droid, my father used to joke.

I think about the complexity of my relationship with my mother now in comparison with this intimate, simple beginning.

I can be cold and distant and angry. We can both be passive-aggressive. It took me far too long to start asking about her story. I once was a part of her and have detangled myself and become a separate being in this ever-evolving union in which she continually has to get used to a new separateness and role in my life. I want to figure things out myself, I don't take her advice, and then I lean on her in very hard times, and I ask her to help me.

Before pregnancy, I'd never noted how hard this might be for her.

My friend Caroline is one of five brothers and sisters. She tells me that her mother has told her that one downside to having daughters is that they don't stop sharing their problems with you once they become adults, relying on you for advice and support. It's taxing and stressful. The sons, she says, tend to leave her out of it. I can see, as the mother of five, why you might—after decades—want to be left out of it.

But I've also heard a mother of twin boys lament, *They don't tell me anything!*

We're generalizing here, of course, about gender.

I am still not fond of infants.

These strange, fleshy beings, red-faced, clinging to their mothers, squeaking and cooing.

Occasionally, the push and roll of your limbs remind me you're a living creature inside me. I become queasy, disturbed.

Other times when you move around in there, I feel a violent and deeply rooted flash of affection.

Every so often, your dad and I lie in the dark and imagine you in the bassinet next to the bed. We feel profound terror. We don't know how to take care of a baby.

I imagine your eyes opening at night—their need swallowing me whole.

❄

In the daytime, your father and I talk to you through the wall of my belly. We aren't scared of you.

I pull his hand to my stomach when you start to move, so he can feel you, so he can understand you're real.

❄

I thought being pregnant with you would make life seem pointful, but it still seems completely pointless. These days, though, that doesn't upset me.

❄

The only sense I can make of life is that there is no sense to it. No purpose.

But you can fill it with what feels like purpose—love, curiosity, conversation, a passion that *feels* like the reason you are here.

That could be writing, like it is for me. That could be making food that brings friends together. That could be playing with numbers, flying planes, or tending to the sick.

That could be making a home.

It's your choice, baby.

I promise to do my best not to project onto you my own desires for your future.

My belly is huge now and it delights your father. The bigger I get the more he is willing to do for me, though by more I simply mean that the thought now occurs to him that I might not want to be lugging my laundry down the icy, outdoor stairs of our apartment to our laundry room, which is in a cellar that can only be accessed from outside.

Maybe I should do your wash, he says, more like a question. The thought actually occurred to our landlord first, who inquired if I was still lugging loads down the treacherous back stairs of his property.

I wonder sometimes who and where these men are you see in movies—the ones who rub their pregnant wives' feet and whisper sweetly to their bellies. That's not your dad and me—we are entirely unsentimental.

I don't want sentimentality, favors, I just want him to acknowledge I'm working really hard over here—I'm powerful.

I tell my midwife I've gained more weight than I think I should have. She says my body must prepare for a famine so you and I would have fat stores to live on. I picture an arctic landscape when she says this, standing with you in a glare of snow.

❄

If a person has what is considered a "normal" body mass index before pregnancy, the Institute of Medicine recommends gaining between twenty-five and thirty-five pounds during pregnancy. I hover near forty, as do most of my close friends during their first pregnancy.

All this stuff about what is "normal" before, during, and after seems problematic.

At a baby shower I attend, everyone writes down a fact about themselves and puts it in a hat. The guest of honor pulls each out and reads them aloud and we are all supposed to guess who the fact belongs to.

One of the facts is that one woman in attendance only gained fifteen pounds during her pregnancy with her child. The guests explode with approval and jealousy when the identity of the author is revealed. She beams with pride.

A colleague informs me he feels women are *delicate flowers* and should be treated as such. We are walking over icy sidewalks toward our workplace when he says this, and I am heavily pregnant with you, my every muscle tensed against a fall, my body a workhorse, loaded with life.

I don't like being pregnant.

I feel guilty admitting this. I have to assure myself, and assure you, that saying this is not the same thing as saying I am not grateful for you, or I don't want you. I do.

But I don't love sharing my body.

After you've lived your life in a body that is yours alone for thirty-four years, it's an adjustment to suddenly be sharing it with another human and it is bizarre that I don't feel comfortable being open about that. Of course it's not comfortable, but that doesn't mean I am not also thrilled to be doing it.

The eternal gratitude of the pregnant woman.

The first thing you should know, said a friend, when our mutual friend was debating if she wanted to get pregnant, *is that you could die.* She herself had faced the possibility.

You babies can kill your mothers upon exit and before exit in multiple ways—preeclampsia, amniotic embolism, hemorrhaging. Maternal death *is* rare in industrialized countries, but it exists, and the fact that it hasn't been addressed worldwide is devastating.

The United States has the worst maternal mortality rates of all the industrialized countries, with roughly 33 women per 100,000 live births dying in 2021. The maternal mortality rate for Black women in the US in the same year was a shocking 69.9 deaths per 100,000 live births. For Hispanic women, it was 28 deaths per 100,000 live births, and for white women, 26.6. The country's rates have only been getting worse.

But pregnancy can lead to so many other serious mental and physical health issues, so many difficult or devastating experiences, like postpartum depression, miscarriage, neonatal loss.

A mother my friend knows dies by suicide when her baby is five months old.

Our friend loses consciousness in her car from overwhelming blood loss caused by a piece of the placenta that stayed lodged in her body after a miscarriage. Luckily, she calls an ambulance before passing out and wakes up on the stretcher.

I know at least twelve other women who've had miscarriages, though not all with such serious complications.

Your dad's colleague loses her baby during labor.

Maybe it's grim to focus on these darker realities of pregnancy, but I want a ritual that recognizes the risk of death and darkness we are taking on when we find out we are growing babies.

Instead, everything is pink and blue balloons, baby bumps, and fun Instagram announcements. I hate this cuteness. It glosses over the profound physical and psychic risks, trespasses, and burdens I'm taking on by carrying you. I find it offensive that the cultural narrative surrounding human gestation is one of preciousness.

I feel like a killjoy.

✳

Maybe everyone's just trying to take our minds off it all.

But maybe it's also an insidious denial of our brawn and courage.

Nights are sleepless.

What if you die, baby?

This is just the beginning. I'm going to worry about you for the rest of my life.

It's all-consuming—the death threat. Like objects and decisions have turned cruel.

If I choose to drive to the store, will I get in an accident and kill you? Is this car safe? What about these stairs? My mental fogginess? This sidewalk covered in ice?

We're at thirty weeks. We're in the home stretch.

Every Monday evening I go to prenatal aquafit at the pool and bob up and down with a dozen other women, their hair in buns. In the showers after I sneak glances at all their bodies. I like to see what their breasts are like, how their bellies protrude, the arch of their backs. I am fascinated by all of them. They look so beautiful: their blue and green veins rising to the surface of their skin as if becoming translucent.

I wish I could see myself this way.

I used to attend this class with a friend, who is four weeks further along than me. The last time we came, she was sitting on the bench in her swimsuit after class and when she stood up, she left a small pool of blood behind. She could feel it and looked down. Her blue eyes opened wide, and a drop fell to the tile between her sandals.

Is that you? I asked. It was a stupid question.

She ran to the bathroom.

At the hospital, they said the baby would need to be cut out as soon as possible, maybe in a week or so, after she'd had a little more chance to develop. My friend would have to stay in a hospital bed until then.

They should both be okay, but I am terrified by the limbo they're in. I keep seeing her blue eyes open wide and that drop of blood, all the women bobbing with their bellies in the pool. The baby doing her own bobbing; a waiting room before life.

Maybe I do not feel a connection to you because of the impossible brutality that still, even now, nothing will ensure your survival.

My friend Rebecca says she has an intimate connection with her baby (who is still in utero).

Maybe I am hesitant to become attached.

When Rebecca talks about this connection, I wonder what she means. You're more concept than anything else. You're still a stranger, even though you've lived inside my body for many months.

We'll have to get to know each other.

It's just another form of waiting, this. I'm good at waiting. I've been doing it all my life.

I have always thought the next stage in my life—the next moment—would be better, and whatever I was doing at the time was filler. I was waiting to grow up. I was waiting to be in university. I was waiting until I was out of university. I was waiting to meet a different man. I was waiting until I lost ten pounds. I was waiting for my next trip abroad. I was waiting for the next job. I was waiting for the night to be over. I was waiting for the gnocchi to be served. I was waiting for my next shot of tequila, my next glass of wine. I was waiting for the party—for the moment I would feel electricity. I was waiting to be pretty, to be thin, to be esteemed. I was waiting until I wasn't so self-conscious. I was waiting for self-confidence, to be the life of the party. I've been waiting.

Now I'm waiting for you.

Your future nursery is my current writing room—I am sitting in it right now. There isn't even a crib in here yet, just my writing desk and my papers. When you arrive, I'll have to share a writing room with your father—not that he works much from home—but still, what will I lose in that reduction?

❄

For now, I think of being in this room with you at night. I think of it being just you and me. I think about the privilege and the beauty of that. Just watching you breathe, be alive, our eyes meeting. The fragrance of you. The night outside.

❄

You will be a separate person soon, one I can look at.

I used to be able to feel you moving much more, and more markedly, but I don't anymore. This often happens with babies at this late stage because they've gotten so big they have less room to maneuver, so their movements are more subtle. But sometimes the baby may actually be moving less, or not at all, which means they're not doing well. It's another one of those impossible things about pregnancy: every symptom, movement, or lack thereof could mean a multitude of things, could mean life or death. No nausea in the first trimester might mean a person's hormones are off and they are about to miscarry, or it might mean everything is perfectly fine and they're lucky.

I talk to my midwife about my fears. She thinks you are doing fine but says she will trust my instincts and send me for an ultrasound.

I go and see you on the screen. You look well, the technician tells me. She estimates you weigh seven pounds twelve ounces. I don't know how she knows this.

BIRTH

Spring

*Under patriarchy, pregnancy and childbirth are savage
"tests" of your ability to survive the wilderness alone.
And to keep quiet about what you've seen.*

—Phyllis Chesler, *With Child: A Diary of Motherhood*

You were born two weeks before you were due.

My water broke late on a Sunday morning. This didn't happen in a gush, like you see in the movies, but as a slow, steady trickle. I took off my pants and stood in the bathtub and watched the liquid run down my thighs, wondering if this was really it or if the weight of you was finally making me incontinent.

I'm not ready for it to happen today, I thought, *today is a beautiful day.* And it was—uncharacteristically warm and sunny for late April. I had plans. After lounging in bed late with your father, I had dressed and grabbed a book by Elena Ferrante and was about to head to the patio of a café nearby to read—and then I felt it.

I called my midwife and she said she'd meet us at the hospital. She told me to have some lunch to get my strength up.

As I ate lunch, your dad rushed around packing bags, saying, *Okay, okay, okay* to himself, *This is it, okay.* We found free parking on a side street because your dad's a little cheap like that, and then we wandered through the corridors of the hospital up to the maternity ward.

I paced the halls. I felt supremely calm. The contractions were manageable. I sat on an exercise ball for a while and, still, the contractions were manageable. I walked around some more. The pain's intensity started to creep in, but still, it was manageable—very, very painful, but in a way I could handle.

And then suddenly—and I don't remember any sort of transition, other than that I became increasingly desperate to squat or be on all fours—it wasn't—*my god* it wasn't—and I was on my knees on the hospital bed, facing the wall, the head of the bed raised, my arms draped over the top. Your dad on one side of me and the midwife on the other and an ultrasound picture of you placed in front of me for "motivation." I didn't scream in pain as I thought I might. The agony sent me so far inside myself I could barely speak. Each contraction was ninety seconds long, peaking in intensity around the forty-five-second point, a black-hole type of pain that erased god. I thought each one might kill me.

They call this phase of labor—when a person's cervix dilates those last few centimeters—transition. It is by far the most painful part—what I imagine to be like passing through the mouth of hell.

❧

I didn't want to get an epidural.

Epidurals can lead to longer labor and more medical intervention. And some women say they can't feel when to push when they've received an epidural—and I like to be in control. I knew epidurals meant decreased mobility as well and I really wanted to be able to get into whichever position I chose.

I also felt I had to prove something to myself, perhaps that I could do what so many women before me had done. My mother had had me without an epidural, as millennia of other women had with their babies. I wanted to belong to them. I wanted to know what they had been through, to feel placed in history with them. I wanted to know what it felt like. (There's another side of me who thinks many of these women would balk at my decision—why not accept the miracle of pain relief that they did not have access to?)

I thought about these other women through the pain, which I can't do justice to with words, which Doris Lessing once described as beyond a state of pain and more of a state of being. I'd always heard women describe childbirth as an unbelievable torture, but somewhere in the back of my brain thought they might be exaggerating.

I can be such a condescending prick sometimes.

I wondered how something so essential to our species' existence could be almost unbearable.

When I sat down to write about this, I knew I might fail to express anything remotely resembling the actual experience.

But I'm trying.

A few hours into contractions, your heartbeat began to drop with each one. My midwife became very worried. She wanted to insert a heart rate monitor that attached to the skin over the crown of your head, which she would do by inserting the device into my vagina and gently threading it through your skin.

Lying on my back for the procedure was agonizing. I'm an animal—I wanted to be on all fours.

Soon after, the midwife told me I needed to start pushing. I couldn't believe it. I couldn't fathom how—when I felt I had already used up every ounce of my energy to survive the agony—I would then somehow have to figure out how to push a baby out of my vagina.

I had to stay on my back because of the heart monitoring device, a position that felt counterproductive to pushing.

I pushed for over an hour and you would not come out. Your heart rate was still dropping wildly with each contraction. Highly concerned, the midwife decided she needed to transfer my care to the obstetrician on duty.

The OB came in with a team of nurses and said we needed to get you out *now*, so she was going to give me an episiotomy—make a small cut to my vaginal opening—to facilitate your arrival. The nurses crowded around my bed.

Fine, I said. I would have let someone cut you out with a rusty butcher knife at that point. But they were going to give me local anesthetic with a needle first and needed to wait for a contraction to pass to give it to me. This saved me. With a contraction on-coming, and the help of a goddamn savior of a nurse who told me to tuck my chin and curl forward like an athlete, I gave one final push—the doctor poised to freeze me—and you crowned.

A few more pushes and you were out—alive—and no episiotomy.

When they put you on my chest, the umbilical cord still attached to you and the placenta inside me, I couldn't really process that you were there. I couldn't really care. I was away from my body. Shocked by what had just transpired.

Your father kept telling me to look at you. So I looked at you.

There you were, Jude. Crying. Covered in vernix. Limbs curled against my chest.

☙

Remember when I worried about you being a boy? What lunacy. I would never have you any other way than exactly how you are.

☙

I did love you right away. Or, at least, I wanted to look and look and look at you.

After labor, I also had to deliver the placenta. It's no fun.

Want to see it? asked my midwife.

Sure, I said, and she wheeled it over on a cart, where it was sprawled on top like a jellyfish. She pointed to it here and there, giving me a lesson.

This thing, baby, is an organ my body grew to keep you alive.

Now my body has no use for it. Some women keep theirs to bury in their gardens or get ground into tablets to ingest. I told her she could take it away.

I also had a small tear in my labia from birthing you. This is common, I'm told, but I'd had no idea. The midwife stitched me up while my labia were still numb and burning from your exit.

I was not exactly thrilled in that moment, but I watched Tess as she worked and was in total awe of her—of her profession, for the way midwives guide women through this harrowing process. She's a medical practitioner who stitches me up and monitors your heart rate, but she's also been there to help counsel me through the anxiety and fear I felt throughout pregnancy.

Through most of history, childbirth was the domain of midwives.

While male physicians were involved in childbirth on and off throughout history, often mostly for difficult or complicated births, in the eighteenth and nineteenth century, doctors in Europe became more involved due to the proliferation of hospitals, the growth of cities, and the invention of things like forceps.

Other medical inventions—such as administering pain relief, which women desperately wanted—made a lot of people believe physician-assisted births were safer, although they wouldn't be until roughly the mid-twentieth century.

In the nineteenth century, doctors would perform autopsies and then attend to labors without washing their hands in between, causing a deadly infection called puerperal fever, otherwise known as childbed fever.

The history of midwifery in Canada and other countries is also closely linked with colonialism. Indigenous communities had a long history of what we would now recognize as midwifery care, but like so many forms of Indigenous knowledge and practice, it was systematically and purposefully destructed by settlers. In the late nineteenth century, Indigenous women were sent out of their home communities by the Canadian government to give birth in distant, federally-run hospitals. This was part of the government's broader plan to assimilate Indigenous people.

In settler communities in Canada as well, childbirth went from the realm of midwives to hospitals in the twentieth century.

The switch of childbirth care from the hands of women into that of doctors was a massive shift in power; men controlled the birth process almost entirely in this new system, and often gave women no choice in the way they experienced birth, including if they wanted drugs. They could be put in a twilight sleep—which was essentially an injection of morphine and scopolamine—which caused a sort of drowsy stupor, though not a total loss of consciousness, and wiped a woman's memories of birthing her child away entirely.

Twilight sleep increased the chance of prolonged labor, the use of forceps, and infant suffocation.

Let me pause here to say that I'm not trying to demonize the medical establishment. The many advancements brought by the medicalization of birth, from germ theory to Caesarian sections have made labor—and childhood—infinitely safer.

I am happy that women now have a choice of medical provider, and I recognize that not all women can have midwifery care, as women with complicated or high-risk pregnancies need to be followed by obstetricians.

I chose midwifery care because it is safe, holistic, and much more focused on giving women the power to make their own choices. With a midwife, I could choose to give birth at a hospital, a birthing center, or at home. I could choose which position I birthed in.

The Public Health Agency of Canada has flagged that the number of women in hospitals "giving birth in a supine position" needs to be improved, as in less women should give birth this way. Being in a position that uses gravity to help push the baby out, such as squatting, is simply more efficient, while giving birth in a supine position has been proven—through over three decades of research—to have significant disadvantages and no benefit to the mother or infant. Women are encouraged to give birth on their backs simply because it is easier for the doctors to catch the babies that way.

I gave birth on my back due to the monitoring device that was inside me, threaded in your skull, but it was not the position my body wanted to birth in.

In undertaking this life-changing process that I had little control over, choice felt important.

Several studies have also established that midwifery care is associated with fewer instrument-assisted births, lower C-section rates, and reduced hospital stays.

The hospital staff asks if we want to go home or stay the night at the hospital. I want to stay because I can't imagine taking you home in this state, us being alone with you. I need someone to care for *me*, make *me* feel safe, after going through what feels like a trauma.

What just happened? I want to ask someone.

I don't sleep all night. I am too wired—high on the magic of you. I just stare at you as you sleep in your little plastic bassinet.

Behind you, your dad is curled up on a little daybed, deep in slumber.

In the bathroom of my hospital room in the maternity ward, there is a sign posted asking:

- Does your partner hit you?
- Is he controlling?
- Does he ever get jealous?
- Is he possessive?
- Are you ever afraid of your partner?

I read these questions each time I got up that first night to change the massive pad I was leaking blood and fluid into, aware of this new life I was responsible for just outside the door, my legs still shaking from the effort of labor. And I thought about the women who answer yes to those questions.

I still think about them.

In the hours after your birth your dad is ecstatic.

This is the happiest day of my life, he says. *You're the most amazing woman in the world.*

I imagine countless men have said this to the women they love in the moments after they've watched them bring children into the world. Here, in these moments, men witness the ferocious grit, strength, and mental fortitude of women.

I imagine that some of these are the same men who believe women can't run corporations or countries, as if this strength is a superpower reserved only for bearing offspring.

When I was nineteen, as I mentioned previously, my lung collapsed spontaneously, a phenomenon called a spontaneous pneumothorax. I was travelling in France at the time.

At first, the hospital staff didn't believe anything was truly
wrong with me—they thought I was having a panic attack. They
even asked if my boyfriend had beaten me up (I had no boyfriend
at the time, so that would have been tricky). Later, after they con-
firmed my oxygen saturation level was low and X-rays showed my
left lung had collapsed, the staff told me they hadn't believed me
because I didn't seem to be in the amount of pain they expected.

Grown men cry when they have this, one of the nurses explained.

Of the very few things I have ever inherited, one of my favor-
ites, is from my aunt Marie, who gave me a collection of medical
textbooks from the early twentieth century that were in the pos-
session of my maternal grandmother when she died. The books
had belonged to my grandfather's grandfather, Frederick George
Burrows.

Frederick was a small-town doctor, I was told, the type who
liked to be paid with a bottle of whiskey.

When perusing a textbook of his entitled *A Manual of
Operative Surgery with Surgical Anatomy and Surface Markings*
from 1913, I came across a section on general conditions to consider when performing surgery. One was a person's sex. The text
read:

> Over a large number of cases it is found that
> women bear operation slightly better than

men. This is probably due to the fact that the average woman lives a quieter and more temperate life than the average man. Women are as a rule more patient of restraint.

It is not that a woman might bear pain better, or be stronger, baby, this author—one Duncan C.L. Fitzwilliams—could not even entertain such a notion.

We're shape-shifters, women—beasts, but everyone likes to hush that up.

When we get home, we place you—still clipped into your car seat—on the living room floor.

Now what?

The cat comes and sniffs at you.

LIFE

Summer

Our society is exceptional in giving mothers primary responsibility for infant care in an isolated domestic setting with exceptionally sharp boundaries, with or without supplementary help from the father, a grandmother, a babysitter, or a child care center.

—Sarah LeVine and Robert A. LeVine, *Do Parents Matter?: Why Japanese Babies Sleep Soundly, Mexican Siblings Don't Fight, and American Families Should Just Relax*

In the first week of your life, Jude, I get all those waves of oxytocin that make a person deliriously high on love—and thank
christ—because without them I would not survive.

I barely sleep. My vulva is swollen and sore. My breasts are
raw from your nonstop feedings.

I can't be away from you for very long—even in sleep—
because you might need to eat.

I've lost my freedom.

My friend Rebecca says that in life, you always give one thing
up for another.

❧

The thing I'm getting is you, which is pleasure and warmth, an
exuberant intoxicating love that finally places me in the right here
and right now.

Such new life strips away the redundancy of the outside world
and I see—for a brief spell—what being alive is, and every detail
that makes up a life, makes you.

And you—you take in every detail of this outside place
you've suddenly found yourself in, and I get to see it all again,
too, for another first time.

❧

You have thick, soft hair, your father's deep, dark blue eyes, and
ample round cheeks. You look like my brother, my father—I can
see the Ukrainian in you from my paternal grandfather's side.

Motherlike

We count your life in hours, then days.

A few days in, your dad and I watch *Midnight Express*. We place you on the couch between us, where you fall asleep. I don't really watch the movie, which is terrible anyway. I think about how you weren't here a few days ago and now you are. It follows that you could also be gone suddenly—the universe might want you back.

I can't bear the idea and feel madly possessive of you, greedy. I already feel like I would not want to live if you weren't here.

How I can love a person who did not exist in the outside world until a few days ago is baffling—the love feels like plummeting.

This sudden and profound vulnerability I now feel is the biggest downside to having a child. When I am in that state between sleep and wake, which is often these days, I think obsessively about your death. Your fragility is terrifying. I am aware how easily something minor could kill you: you could stop breathing in your crib, be strangled by a cord, swallow a button from your shirt. My mind constantly scans for danger.

Just writing this, I am uneasy, like writing about it is bad luck. I have become deeply superstitious in motherhood.

My own mother was the same way when her babies arrived. She didn't christen me because she was worried that god might take me if she did now that I was his. This is a barely religious woman I am talking about, a "convenient Christian," as my father once called her.

My mother rarely mentioned god to me growing up. Religion was always presented as a lovely spectacle; we occasionally went to church when we visited my mother's mother in the small hamlet she lived in. The church was tiny and old—I'd run my fingers over the worn bibles in the back of the pews and wonder over the stained-glass windows, how these people all knew what to say and sing, the ivory candles, the dust dancing in the light, the feeling that being here was somehow special, that I was special. My mother stood next to me and sang in her terribly sweet but terribly off-tune voice, her black hair shiny in the streaming sunlight. I wanted to be in the god-believing club only because it was so foreign yet so welcoming. Something mystical, like you.

That my mother believed so powerfully in this entity she seemed to rarely interact with only made sense to me once you were born.

If death is simply obliteration, yours would be mine.

In understanding our vulnerability I've also come to be in awe of life. I don't mean in a religious sense, I mean that cells multiplying, evolution—it is all such a mind-blowing miracle.

Sustaining new life takes a type and level of work that was previously unfathomable to me.

My midwife tells me I have to wake you up every three hours during the night to breastfeed you. It takes you forty-five minutes to feed, which means I only sleep for roughly two hours before I must get up again. My iPhone alarm is littered with the oddest wake-up times: 1:20 a.m., 3:45 a.m., 4:15 a.m.

No one told me about this absurd nocturnal schedule the entire time I was pregnant.

Can this be right?! I want to scream at nobody in particular. *I need sleep! My body just produced a baby!*

They do this to new mothers to ensure the baby is eating enough and does not starve to death, which is indeed possible. Apparently, Jude, you might sleep through fatal hunger.

The weight of the decision to breastfeed exclusively, a scenario in which my body alone keeps you alive, where my absence means your hunger, is crushing.

I'd always imagined breastfeeding would be magically easy; I would place you at my breast and you would just know how to draw out the milk. It would be relaxing and intimate.

That's not how it is for you and me. And it turns out breastfeeding is anything but simple for many women, which is why there are lactation consultants, experts at getting babies to latch onto women's nipples correctly or diagnosing and solving other breastfeeding difficulties. In the weeks after your birth, I sought their help, sitting in numerous community centers (where many work) with my breasts exposed to a group of women waiting their turn, while a consultant showed me the complex movement of shoving you onto my breast at exactly the right angle at exactly the right point during the action of your mouth opening. The nipple has to hit the palate of your mouth. Your chin has to be tucked. Your upper lip has to cover most of my areola. It's a science.

The first time I go to a group consult with a lactation expert you are only three days old.

Another mom asks me how old you are.

You are already such a good mother, she tells me, *to care so much that you came here.*

I almost start crying. Sometimes the brilliant kindness of women breaks me right open.

She knew I needed to hear someone say this, perhaps having experienced the notion herself that not being able to breastfeed with ease can read in a mother's mind like failing.

After consultations with more than five different lactation experts, I'm told there isn't really a problem. They tell me my nipples are sensitive and need to get used to a baby feeding from them—and you need to grow and get a bigger mouth.

Meanwhile, the consultants are militant that I don't stop breastfeeding and that I never give you a bottle of pumped milk or formula because you may come to prefer it.

Prefer it!

Their tone implies preferring a bottle would be a horrid outcome. One consultant recognizes my desperation and tells me that if I really can't handle this anymore, I could try spooning drops of milk into your mouth until you are full, a process I imagine would take hours. I find their lack of flexibility cruel. The pain is difficult enough to deal with at three p.m. but becomes nightmarish at three a.m. I realize very quickly that the only reason I can continue breastfeeding is all the support I have.

Without it, I would not be able to do this.

An older couple comes to visit. At some point during their stay, I breastfeed you. The husband exclaims in approval, grumbling about a mutual friend who recently had a baby, too, and had decided not to breastfeed.

I'm so glad you're doing what's best for your baby, he says.

The woman he's talking about is a single mother and a business-owner.

His wife turns to him: *You have no idea what you're talking about.*

There are well-publicized benefits to exclusively breastfeeding, but I firmly believe there are more benefits to having a mother who isn't so stressed and exhausted that she is coming apart.

Your dad begs me to quit or at least to let him give you the occasional bottle. He says I'm about to lose my mind. But I won't give up, because as much as I believe that a mother's sanity is more important, I know I'd feel weak and guilty if I quit. I would never think this way about another woman, but I think this way about myself. I don't know if this is a sneaking sense of superiority—a subconscious conviction that I am more than human, or if I am just harder on myself than I am on other women.

Whatever the reason, I believe I owe an apology to other mothers for acting this way, because not giving myself a break or allowing myself to do only what I find reasonable helps maintain the pressure on other women to do the impossible and preserves that sense of destructive competition women can have with each other.

It's often about bodies, this competition.

Who is slimmer, or whatever.

And now, here we are, the mothers, alone in our dwellings, in invisible competition with each other again, but now it's about how we go about keeping our infants alive in a way that's in keeping with the current standards of what it means to be feminine, to be *good women*.

The difficulty is that, in this mix, there is you. What belongs to my concern for your well-being, my belief in what is best for you, confuses the issue. Am I killing myself to breastfeed for your health, for the sake of what others think of me, how they value me, or both?

I know I partly do it to please the neurotic in me, who notes that breast milk has been proven to help babies develop a strong immune system, so if you ever get sick, baby, I could tell my neurotic it wasn't my fault—I did everything I could.

No matter what, it feels like it's always going to be my fault.

In a 1987 *Washington Post* article entitled "Haven't We Blamed Mother Long Enough? Common Explanations for Children's Emotional Problems are a Trap," psychologist Paula J. Caplan writes about the findings from a review of hundreds of articles published in respected mental health journals over the span of twelve years.

In 125 of the articles, mothers were held responsible for 72 different types of psychological disorders in their children, ranging from agoraphobia to hyperactivity to schizophrenia. Not one of these articles described a mother as "emotionally healthy," though dads were described as such, nor were any mother-child relationships described as "ideal," though some father-child relationships were described as such.

As Caplan wrote, "As long as mothering is assumed to be the only or primary cause of children's psychopathology, then all that remains to be done is to figure out which kind of bad mothering is to blame."

As Harriet Lerner notes in *The Dance of Anger*, even when men get angry, our epithets to describe them—bastard, son of a bitch—put the blame on their mothers.

I start breaking out into hives, sometimes in the middle of the night, sometimes in the afternoon. I've never broken into hives before.

The midwife says I might be allergic to my own breastfeeding hormones, which is a relatively unstudied phenomenon researchers believe may be caused by the combination of a rise in prolactin, a hormone that stimulates breast milk—and oxytocin—and a drop in progesterone, a hormone that increases during pregnancy then drops off after. The reaction could get so bad I'd go into anaphylactic shock. I have trouble understanding how this could be a thing.

I lie awake during the attacks, trying to still my breathing, itchy and hot under the sheets. I stand in the bathroom and splash cool water on my face. I try to get back to sleep before I must feed you again. Luckily, the outbreaks stop after a week.

This postpartum shit is more insane than all nine months of pregnancy combined.

I come to dread bedtime because I know it will be nothing but a brutal series of wake-ups from desperately needed slumber, of sessions of attempting to stay conscious in a nursing chair, reminding myself that succumbing to the sweet pull of sleep might mean dropping a tiny, soft-skulled bundle.

I listen to podcasts and do online banking. Anything to keep me awake.

Real sleep—uninterrupted sleep—is a place of warm shadows, a haven I want to go to forever. These fragments of unconsciousness are physically painful—I tumble in, drag myself out.

Your dad sleeps through everything. I resent him for it.

You cry and he sleeps. You whimper and I wake. I nudge him with my foot forcefully and he gets up and changes your diaper, but you still need to eat.

I want to be the one who gets to sleep through everything.

By doing MRI scans of parents' brains after they've interacted with their children, researchers have discovered that more areas of the brain responsible for being attuned to danger, such as the amygdala, light up in the primary caregiver—often the mother, though it also happens in one partner in same-sex male couples—than in the brain of the secondary caregiver.

In other words, I'm hardwired to sleep lightly.

What's the baby like? someone asks me.
God, I don't know. You're barely alive yet.
Your personhood has only just begun.

❦

The same person asks, *What's good about mothering? I can only see the things that are hard.*

What can I tell her? I understand this must look like a mess. I remember from before how it looked from the outside.

Maybe I could tell her that despite all the overwhelming challenges, I want to put my face to the floor and say thank you to whatever force or chance has allowed me to be the mother of the stunning, glorious child that is you—you who has let me feel this unconditional love. I would not have known it otherwise.

As a non-believer, there's nowhere else to channel that gratitude except into the grains of the wooden floor, the threads of my sheets, the thick, sandy hair on your head.

Thank you, my sweet boy, thank you.

You're over a month old now. You do a thing that looks like smiling when you're full of milk. You toss your arms up over your head when you sleep. The warmth and feel of you against me is so enchanting and necessary, it seems impossible that you weren't always here.

There's a desire to absorb you.

I notice that women who've been through labor recently want to talk about it.

I want to talk about it.

I want to tell each person who comes to visit every little detail I can remember about pushing you out of my vagina. I know this is really weird. I acknowledge that. It must seem an incredibly private, even inappropriate, experience. Plus, everyone already knows the ending.

However, if a person has been through it, they know the drama of it, they realize how many strange turns it can take, how each labor differs wildly. How harrowing and tumultuous and sensational it is. How privacy gets pushed to the side. How one moment they had a body that did all the normal things it always did—ran, ate, fucked, danced, aged, ached, slept, etcetera, and then it created another human and pushed it out into the world, taking them along for the ride.

When my uterus began forcefully contracting in order to open and shorten my cervix and move you down toward the world, it did so on its own. I had no say in it. It was a hurricane I had to survive.

What an animal, this body of mine, raging bear.

❦

It turns out not many people want to hear about your birth. I force the details on them anyway. I need to tell my story.

I'm also ravenous for others', so I start asking.

My maternal grandmother's labor with her firstborn—my uncle George—was very fast. The hospital was not expecting it to happen so quickly, so they didn't call the doctor early enough.

She felt the urge to push and started, but the nurses held her legs together. *Only the doctor can catch the baby*, they told her.

My mother says my uncle suffered permanent facial nerve damage as a result, which presents as a slight droop in his facial features on one side.

After, when she breastfed, which she felt was more natural, the doctor clucked at her, disapproving.

My other grandmother tells me the story of giving birth to my father. She went into labor four and a half weeks before her due date. When she arrived at the hospital, they strapped her to the bed by securing her arms to the rails. She was then put into twilight sleep. Just like that, my grandmother's memories of her first child's birth were erased.

Afterward, no one thought to offer her the chance to see her baby.

She didn't lay eyes on him for days. She was only eighteen years old and was too polite to ask. When a visiting pediatrician finally inquired about what she thought of him, she burst into tears and confessed she'd never even seen him, which prompted outrage from the doctor and my dad's immediate collection.

I wonder what they did with my father during those first days—who touched him, who loved him, who cooed to him. Did he realize he had not yet met his mother?

Are you my mother?

Raising a child at eighteen was very difficult, this grandmother says, *I was too young.*

Seven years later, when she had a second child, my grandfather's appendix burst shortly before she went into labor. While she gave birth to the baby, he recovered in a hospital bed on a different floor. She went home alone with my aunt and cared for the two children on her own. This was even harder than the first time—so hard her thoughts went dark. A doctor diagnosed her with postpartum depression and put her on medication, something she is still incredibly grateful for. He did not stigmatize her, he did not hesitate; he was kind and understanding, saying anyone in her situation would be struggling.

I'm so grateful for this doctor in a time when they could be terrifying to women.

In years past, when the daughter of this grandmother—my aunt—wasn't doing well—suffering from decades of chronic migraines, mind clouded by a haze of drugs an ill-informed doctor prescribed to alleviate them—she occasionally criticized my grandmother, blaming her for the fact her life didn't turn out the way she wanted. My grandmother's succinct response was *I did my best*—a statement she returned to over and over.

On days when I am not sure I am enough for you, I think about this.

After your father's maternal grandmother had her fourth child and was still in hospital recovering, she asked the doctor for a hysterectomy. She didn't want any more children.

In those days, a woman needed her husband's signature in order to get the procedure. Her husband hesitated. A nurse shoved the documents at him, *Sign the goddamn papers*, she scowled. And so he did.

My mother said childbirth wasn't *that* painful. *I mean, you do it, and then it's done*, she said.

She said the obstetrician and your grandfather had the ball game playing on the radio in the delivery room during labor with me.

At first, I'm irritated by this, that these men were listening to the ball game, but then my mother explains that it helped her to have something else to focus on. She was listening too.

That is so my mother.

Rebecca gave birth to her daughter on the exact same date I gave birth to you.

Days-long, her labor was excruciating and knocked the joy out of her. When her baby finally arrives, she doesn't immediately feel a connection to her as she did while she was in utero and sinks into a brief depression.

Very briefly after labor, I felt powerful and beautiful in my strength and ability to make a life. I thought this body was marvelous. I felt its usefulness as a working, pumping machine. I felt glorious.

The feeling dulled.

After a month, I was furious at the soft swell of my belly. I started doing YouTube workouts for my core at a frantic pace before you'd wake for the next breastfeeding session. I went to very intense spinning classes that would leave me dizzy, having to pump a bottle of milk for your dad to give you before leaving.

I was also increasingly feeling the femininity and success of my body was not only tied to its aesthetic appearance, but to your growth as well, to my body's ability to breastfeed you with ease and naturalness (which is hard to pull off, especially because you grumble in complaint when you don't feel the milk is coming out fast enough). To my ability to rock and cuddle and sing sweetly to you.

And so, what then—what am I saying about motherhood and bodies?

I don't know. I am saying, at least, that I mourn when you are at my breast sometimes, thinking about how I have never really felt as if my body belongs to me.

Before you, I was always thinking about how men saw it, or perhaps more accurately, I was always thinking about how women saw how men saw it. Now, I'm always thinking about how other women see me performing these physical acts of motherhood: if I look at home in these motions, if I make it look like this is not a performance—like this all comes natural to me (it doesn't)—I have the sense then that my value might go up. Your father's grandmother might think I'm a good woman, for example.

I'm not after this value consciously, but there's a voice going in the back of my head.

It is difficult to reconcile the feminist I claim I am, the one who doesn't give a shit about fitting the typical definition of femininity, with this part of me that hopes other people will see me as a graceful, natural mother.

A natural mother, what's that? I've never been a mother before.

Your dad's grandmother tells me she never breastfed because the doctor told her she was *too hysterical* for it.

Our bodies are not worthy and, also, somehow, we aren't worthy of our bodies.

One day I'm taking a bath with you, my body in its postpartum state, and I see you see me without judgment—you gaze at my naked flesh without positive or negative assessments, just *seeing*.

Seeing me.

I've never been looked at without a value judgment, without criticism or comparison or sexual desire.

You're genuinely just observing.

It's a type of love I've never felt before, one where my body's appearance truly doesn't matter.

I know it won't last—but what a gift.

Before you were born, I read a lot on the internet and in books about how I would have no sexual appetite in the weeks and possibly months after labor.

I think of myself as an intensely sexual person; I have always felt keenly at home in my lust. I've been in more than one relationship where the sex was too infrequent—it led to the relationship's end. I am often turned on or sexually charged during my day-to-day tasks. Sometimes, when I worked in a bar and had the key to open the place myself to start prepping for a shift, I'd be so turned on—for no particular reason, really, other than because the air was heavy with an approaching rainstorm perhaps—that I would have to go into a bathroom stall and get myself off. All to say, the idea of not wanting sex was discomfiting.

As it turns out, my desire did not go away postpartum. The experience of giving birth was both traumatic and astounding, and there's a high that comes with going through the extraordinary. The high makes your dad and I want to touch each other. But I don't want penetration—the idea is frightening, sickening, so fresh is the memory of the pain and entirely alien experience in that space.

I need a transition back to that, so your dad's fingers find me gently, and I am there again in that refuge.

Nevertheless, when you came into our lives, your dad and I did lose a piece of us.

We lost versions of each other that are spontaneous and unencumbered by the responsibility of raising another human being.

One evening we are out pushing you in the stroller, and I became fixated on the idea that he and I will never be able to just jump on our bikes and ride down to the river together, as we often do on summer evenings. We'd have to plan for this outing and get a babysitter for you. This sounds like a small thing, but seizing moments of pleasure together has always been a key characteristic of our relationship.

But now *you* are the primary source of our pleasure. It's a shift more than a loss.

It's easy now for me to see why relationships fail in the presence of children. This is so exhausting. This is so much work. There is so much less time and energy for us as a couple.

There are elements of your care to argue over.

We can't laze in each other's arms on weekend mornings.

There's always your tiny body to care for first, to put before anything else.

There are a million more practical considerations.

And I'm so fucking tired. Sometimes, when you cry out and I'm yanked from the deepest sleep, knowing only I can make you stop, I feel an unparalleled rage at your dad. Perhaps it's not rational, perhaps it is.

And then most of my brain, most of my thoughts, are trained on you.

Blinders on a horse.

And still, the breastfeeding. The time the breastfeeding requires. It is no longer painful, but it goes on and on, night and day.

Right now, you're experiencing a growth spurt and doing something called "cluster feeding," which basically means drinking my milk nonstop.

I feel like I'm on call. If I take a nap or have a shower or go for a walk around the block, I know I might be needed back at any point because you decide you need more milk.

When I do go for short walks, I feel so free. I stare at the world in wonder: how beautiful the night sky and all the people out here living.

Am I living?

I feel, once again, like an animal—everything else ripped off and away from me: the veneer of the job, the night outs with your dad, the work on my next project, long nights of conversations over beer.

I'm just flesh: breasts, milk, belly, arms, eyes. Blinking.

Cows. That's what they compare us mothers to, baby.

And I do feel like one occasionally, sitting here with you latched to my nipple in the dark. Heavy with earth. My feet on the cold floor. Oozing.

Certain friends and family are uncomfortable when I breastfeed in front of them.

I hate when anyone is uncomfortable with it and I hate that I care (not that I ever stop or cover up, I just hate that I am sensitive to others' discomfort). I feel like I've always adopted other people's discomfort as my own, felt responsible for putting others at ease, but I can't do that while also keeping a small baby alive with my milk. I'm so tired. I just want to stop giving a shit.

I blush though sometimes, when I see people shifting in their seats, looking around the room toward anything but us.

Stop blushing, Katherine. You prude.

One of your uncles works for a bank. Once, while we're hanging out and I'm feeding you, he tells me that a client breastfed in his office the other day.

Uh huh? I say.

And she was really attractive.

So? I say.

I DON'T KNOW! he exclaims, shrugging.

A friend tells me about breastfeeding at a small dinner party with her first child.

Whoa, boobs! yelled her friend's boyfriend when she pulled down her top.

When you are nursing, your face in profile reminds me of my father's.

The first time I go out with you in the stroller to a coffee shop, I suffer an identity crisis.

This isn't me, I think. *I'm not the woman with the stroller!* I notice that young women avoid looking at the woman with the stroller—for them, she doesn't exist, she's a representation of a reprehensible choice that is a long, long way away. I remember feeling like them—feeling some sort of loathing for the women with their babies, so I can't blame them. But I'd like to stop and tell them that I haven't become a vacant droid—that I still think and feel outside of you; I think wanting to tell them this has more to do with my own shit than it has to do with them.

I struggle with the door of the coffee shop and the maneuvering of the stroller. Everyone inside watches but no one helps.

I sip my coffee and pray you won't wake up and cry. If you cry, everyone will look at me. I'll ruin their peace. I realize there is probably some sort of etiquette dictating which coffee shops you can enter when you're a woman with a stroller, and which you shouldn't, but I don't know it yet—I came to my usual coffee shop, where everyone is typing on their laptops. I used to type on my laptop.

We leave as soon as I've gulped down my coffee. On the way out, a young man helps me with the door; I'm so grateful I could cry.

Fuck. Here I am in my saccharine femininity: caregiving, breast-feeding, unconditional loving.

I still love my non-mother self; I do not think her life without kids would be any better or any worse. I know she would lead a rich and compelling existence.

I also think this one—this mother version—is leading a rich and compelling one. But I don't think I have known that as a way we talk about motherhood.

When you are two-and-a-half-months-old, your father and I go visit some friends for dinner. When we leave, we place you in your car seat and forget to strap you up. We only realize once we get home and go to take you out.

We just look at each other.

It starts to creep into my head that you are a boy, and boys, often, become men.

They're just babies when they start out, my friend Brecken says, pointing to you and her own baby boy while we're out for gelato and coffee one day, *innocent babies.*

We're discussing a recent case of sexual harassment in the news.

Something goes wrong, she says. *Society teaches them it's okay.*

I look at you sleeping peacefully in your stroller. I want to cry.

You took my last name.

Taking only your father's last name strikes me as a strange idea.

I wanted you to take either mine or both of ours. Your dad didn't like the aesthetics of hyphenation and was more than happy to give you mine, saying he considered it a chance to right the wrong of men giving women and children their names for so many centuries.

This practice has its roots in the fact that women and children were once a man's physical property, to treat and do with as he wished, his actions protected by law. He could sell them or beat them or rape them and, yes, I know this is no longer the case, but the practice is a remnant from that time, a signifier. I know many women do not view it this way—they know it does not mean this for their families. I, however, can't ignore how it symbolically erases my essential part in the equation.

※

The choice to give you my name pained your father's father, who called it lopsided and told us in an email shortly after your birth that it meant your dad was nothing but a sperm donor. He telephoned multiple members of his extended family to complain. I told him no one would have called it lopsided or referred to me as *nothing but a receptacle* if we'd given you only your father's last name. I suppose he did not see the absurdity in that.

After hearing the news, the second wife of one of your great uncles calls me a *nasty woman* on Facebook, one who forced your *poor* dad into this arrangement.

She clearly does not know your father, who would never let himself be forced into any arrangement.

You see, baby, people often accept and even champion inequality when it comes in the form of tradition. They use tradition as the reason to keep doing the inequality.

Traditions can be frightening.

Your grandfather told your dad, *For the sake of continuity, maybe one of your brothers will give me a grandson with my last name.*

Continuity. He wants to live beyond his life—and I'm his opportunity to do so. It gives me secret pleasure to consider how he depends on women's bodies—even that of a nasty woman—for his immortality.

❊

But no, my love, I'm not going to be polite this time.

You will remain named after the body that was once your home.

❊

The anger I feel, dear Jude. Do mothers share their anger with their sons?

They should and must—because it's glorious.

Your father is worried when I get angry in front of you. He worries it traumatizes your growing brain.

But the fighting, our fighting, it's not constant, it's not violent. And we make up and work it out.

And so I am not so worried.

This is what it's like to be human, to be a woman.

I do worry about the expectation on new mothers with partners to be even-keeled, patient, and kind in this time of such intense sleep deprivation and physical and mental demand. It's completely unrealistic.

My friend Katie is as calm as they come. She and her husband are the kindest, most even-tempered, and least fight-y couple I know, but she confided in me that after her son was born, her husband came to her one day, months in, and said that all her sharp comments and snapping was getting to him, hurting his feelings. She essentially told him he was just going to have to deal with it for a while, explaining about the lack of sleep and the cling-on that clawed at her nipples all night.

You're just going to have to let me be a bitch for the time being, she told him.

As mothering goes on, relentless, I miss the luxury of wasting time.

You must get things done while he's in his crib, I tell myself.
Laundry/writing/exercise/dinner.

I'm lonely.

I only have two other friends in this city who currently have small babies. One is already back at work and the other meets up with me a few times a week, which feels essential but is not enough.

Many moms join groups for new parents to combat the isolation. Parent and baby yoga. Story time at the library. Mom and me fitness classes.

I go, too, but I can't find my home in these groups. I'm awkward and uncomfortable and I don't feel like myself. The instructors focus the conversation on mothering only, and although this makes perfect sense—it is what brought us all to that room, after all—it is also reducing. In these spaces, we are all that one-dimensional woman I feared that day my cousin and I went to the beach. We feel obliged to talk about nap schedules and baby-led weaning, as if social mores dictate that content, and although that is now extremely relevant to my day-to-day existence, I need more. I want to be surrounded by people who knew me before this, who knew that I wasn't always struggling to fold up a stroller, drowning in diaper bags, obsessed with sleep routines, covered in spit up. I was and am more than that. This is just one period of my life.

And there is my mother, your grandmother, too far for me to rely on regularly, too far to allow to help do the mothering.

I am stranded.

Most other mothers I know say they feel that way too.

The structured environment of a yoga class or coffee date is not enough. We need some sort of communal place of napping and feeding and being together with our babies, day in and day out. We need to be together in the monotonous. We need an extended network stepping in to rock the baby, make the meals, change the diapers.

But I don't have that. So here we are, Jude, you and I, mostly alone together at three months.

Sometimes you won't stop crying and I can't figure out why. The only thing that soothes you is holding you while I walk the house in circles. If I sit down, you cry, so I have to walk, walk, walk. If I try to put you in the stroller so I can at least walk outside, an activity we spend an extraordinary amount of time doing anyway, you start to wail again. You want to be in my arms. You won't even accept the embrace of a carrier.

Other mothers tell me that babies tend to get less fussy after three months.

Three months pass.

Or maybe it's four, my mother tells me, when I say you seem to have gotten worse.

It's four, says Brecken, *it's definitely four.*

At five, I can't say that it's much better, that you're any less demanding.

Some days I think I can't do this; how can I keep doing this? I'm going to collapse. But I keep going.

It seems wrong, all the lonely doing. All the sleep deprivation. The entire burden. Like a recipe for madness and disaster.

When your father gets home, I shove you at him.

Where has he been, your father?

He's been to the outside world without us.

Every morning I want to tell him, don't leave us. Don't exist in the place of work, the one everyone seems to have agreed has greater value.

Don't come back to us seen, saturated with meaning, while we've been invisible.

※

One of us needs to work during this time. I know this. It could be me. I could let your dad take the whole parental leave.

But I don't want to go back to work yet. I don't want to be without you. I don't want to be anywhere that doesn't acknowledge this is the real world—you—the way my body exists to be close to yours. At times, our small world is the only thing I need.

Still, while I don't want to separate from you, I wish I did not have to be so separated from the world in domesticity.

Our bodies perspire through the summer together, your flesh always searching for mine.

After a long, hard day during the first hot months of your life, you and your father and I crowd into the small attic bedroom of our apartment, where the air conditioner is housed. It's our only respite from the heat and going there feels like an absolute luxury—the three of us in bed reading books, my beautiful man and my beautiful baby. I feel like I've never known such splendor—and I'm not sure I'll ever know it again.

AUTONOMY

Autumn and Winter

*My body, my life became the landscape of my son's life.
I am no longer merely a living thing in the world; I am
a world.*

—Sarah Manguso, *The Two Kinds of Decay*

At six months old, you learn to sit up by yourself and you suddenly become happier and easier to deal with. I sit you down on our wooden floors and prop pillows behind you (your big head still tends to tip you over), and place pots and pans and spoons in front of you. You stir and tap and tip. I make pasta and I put some records on. This is better.

Maybe all you wanted was some autonomy.

I like autonomy too, kiddo.

I feel like your captor sometimes—dictating everything—what you see, eat, touch, and wear. Where we go.

At the same time, I feel like you're *my* dictator. My days revolve around your desires.

Often, I'm just grasping at this—my role as your mother. Am I creating the moments you need to thrive? Is being together and flitting between boredom and play, delight and frustration, enough?

Your eyes show me this world is perplexing, wondrous, and striking, and I'm trying to show up. I'm so exhausted, so weary of the moments, but at some point I get there. I see.

The shadows moving across that wall.
The colors and pattern of this rug.
The way the cat shakes himself out when he's wet.
How our limbs arc through the air.
The endless expressions our faces can make.
The sounds coming from our throats, creating meaning,
connecting us.
Our skin touching, the pleasure of it, like coming home.

Thank you, Jude—for all this, for showing me the details I'd forgotten.

We read a lot.

Ever since you could focus your eyes, you were enthralled by text of any kind.

We read you the *New Yorker* and *Poetry* magazines, the sides of cereal boxes, Robert Munsch, Jessica Love, Eula Biss, and newspapers. I didn't know at first that not all babies are fascinated with letters on a page like you are, mesmerized by stories. I'm grateful because even if you have nothing else, baby, you will always have books.

Your books are full of animals. All the animals are male. Even the inanimate objects are male. When there are real children in the stories, they are male and they are white. I'm worried about you thinking you are the hero of every story, the base point.

I have to search to create a balance, to make sure that most of the stories we read feature diverse characters. I'm constantly changing pronouns. I want to use books to help you empathize with people who don't look like you. It shouldn't be this hard to find enough of them.

Occasionally, I throw a book to the ground, furious at it.

Why do all the mother bears in the stories wear aprons?

Babies think their mothers are the coolest. It's a fact. What I love about this is that you think everything I do is hilarious. For someone who has never been considered funny by anyone else, this is glory.

I ride it for all it's worth. I'm a fool. You get giddy with my stupid silliness.

My brother and I were like this together when we were small. Making idiotic faces and noises at each other, a crude insular sense of humor. I thought I'd lost that when we grew up.

But here we are now—you and I—being very immature. Being ourselves.

You laugh wildly at our antics, fast, like someone's chasing you.

I wander the house with you like I did as a child. Getting into things here, then things there. A trail of boredoms and moments of deep pleasure.

I document the gap in your tooth on Instagram, our domestic life together. We're pictures inside an apartment, walks nearby. We become a series of boxes.

☽

Will you resent me for these public pictures? That I've documented your life for my audience of friends and family, made a narrative of it?

☽

Posting these pictures and captions on Instagram makes me feel less alone in this *isolated domestic setting*.

It makes me feel seen. It's another story I'm telling, one people can respond to.

And what about this book, will you hate that I've written it?

After a time of these days and their endless repetition, rituals, and struggles—our story is changing. I am going back to work.

I have been home with you for nine months. Now your father is taking over for a three-month parental leave.

I am ready for this change because I don't always know what to fill our days with anymore. I get bored. I'm ready because I need to feel another way.

I am excited to get dressed and leave you, then come back to you.

⁂

Reentering work feels like coming back from the dead, like everything was moving and I was still, or like I was moving and everything else was still.

Work also hands me back a sense of myself apart from you. I am not your mom at the office, at least not outwardly. Inwardly, I am forever just your mom.

Even though I have a demanding job, work seems easy compared to caring for you. In the office, I can make myself a coffee without having to simultaneously hold, jiggle, or sing to you. I can take sips at my desk and stare at the wall and have my own thoughts. I can focus.

I feel energized to be my own person again, to be independent of you.

⁂

My manager at work tries to ease me back into this, gives me menial tasks like arranging the office bookshelf, even though I usually do research and writing.

I am worried she thinks I have lost my brains to the baby.
I still have them, I want to tell her, *I swear.*

When I get home from my first day back to work—feeling demoted, your dad reports he had to pull two of those small stickers they put on fruit out of your mouth, but that otherwise the day went smoothly.

He has dinner ready for me and the house is sparkling.

We eat together, then I hang out with you for twenty minutes, and then it's already bedtime. How little we suddenly see of each other. I'm heartbroken; I feel like I'm breaking up with you, but I don't want to.

At work, I pump milk because I don't want to stop breastfeeding you yet, so I pump to keep up my supply. If I didn't, my breasts would get heavy and sore and start to leak every few hours anyway.

Here, my lactating breasts make me feel as if they are sending the message to my colleagues that my body—my female body—rules me. Before, I could pretend as if my femaleness did not intrude in this space unless I welcomed it to, which felt important, as I don't see any evidence that the world trusts female bodies.

My boss wants me to pump in the bathroom. He has someone set up a table and chair in there.

No, I say to the colleague who leads me there.

Instead, she sends me to an empty office with a lock on the door.

After, I wrap the bottle of milk in a plastic bag and put it in the back of the employee fridge. I feel like a freak.

And so, I go from demeaned, underappreciated role of mother at home to working mother. There, at work, I find the other working mothers.

We nod at each other. We know. This solidarity here—it is crucial.

*

I used to stay late at work to prove something. I ambled home at seven, wanting to show my dedication.

Now, I rush out at five, slipping past my boss's office. I need to get home to you.

Does this mean I work less now, have sacrificed the quality of what I produce? *God no.* I've learned efficiency and focus. I don't chat twenty-two times a day in the kitchen like I did before. I don't browse my phone. I'm one of the first in the office, killing it while it's still quiet.

These past nine months I've mastered multitasking like I never have before—I've learned how to prioritize—I've learned how to zone out distractions and focus intensely.

These skills *do* translate to the workplace—being a mother has made me better at work, and when, eight months after my return, I request and receive a large raise, I know everyone—even that big boy boss of mine—has realized it.

*

I know this experience is not typical—being valued at work while you're also a mother.

Numerous studies in the US have found that mothers are less likely to be hired for a job than childless women and men, and fathers. Their pay also decreases four per cent with each child they have, while a man's increases six per cent with each child.

As a *New York Times* article called "The Motherhood Penalty vs. the Fatherhood Bonus" noted, "One of the worst career moves a woman can make is to have children. Mothers are less likely to be hired for jobs, to be perceived as competent at work or to be paid as much as their male colleagues with the same qualifications."

In Canada, the motherhood penalty also exists. Women with children earn twelve per cent less on average than women without children, and that gap grows with each child.

When they're hiring these fathers, I imagine they're assuming the mothers pick up the children from day care or school. They're assuming the mothers take on the brunt of the emotional care, the homework, the extracurriculars, the cleaning that saps any parent's mental energy. They're assuming, in sum, that fathers do not take on an equal amount of parenting and that mothers can't carry the mental load of both.

During this time, I come to understand what it is like to have a wife.

At first, your dad is thrilled to be in this role—*free of work* is how he puts it. But then some time passes. You won't nap, he tells me. The house is always a mess—the baby makes a mess. He accuses me of not pulling my weight and—somewhat childishly—I can't help but revel in the accusation—an accusation that usually comes from my mouth.

During dinner one night, you accidentally drop some food from your high chair, and he gets down on his hands and knees right in the middle of dinner and starts to scoop it off the floor, muttering vehemently. You and I just watch him, aghast.

I empathize with him, but I also feel grateful that he's experiencing what so many mothers have, which is that all day we entertain and care for the child(ren), with zero breaks, dealing with hunger and mood swings and accidents and shit. Juggling the baby's emotions and our own—constantly comforting, calming, teaching, safeguarding.

We attempt to put the house—or something, anything—in order, while also entertaining the baby, and then we watch it all get undone, over and over again, as the baby throws his food on the floor, dumps the contents of a shelf, scatters his toys everywhere, clings to our bodies. Dinner might involve balancing the baby on one hip and stirring scalding pasta with the other, and when dad gets home he can't see any of that—it produces no visible, concrete result. He talks about his day, with all the importance of the outside world attached to it, and we don't seem to have anything important to say as we've just been bending, chasing, protecting, scrubbing, reading, playing, and managing all day. In our society, there is no real value placed on caring for children.

I'm sorry, I've just been raising this beautiful human. It's nothing, really.

This is enough to make anyone—even a man—absolutely fucking crazy.

There are moments in my workday when I think of our world at home—the intimacy you and I created, how I lost myself in the pleasure of play, in the pleasure of you.

I miss it, but I don't want to return there, and yet I wonder if I would if everyone acted like what I was doing there with you was as important as it really is.

Lost in work, there are also moments when I don't think about you. I didn't think that was possible.

Still, baby, you sit in my bones. You possess a section of my brain. You never leave me, even when my thoughts are elsewhere.

I learn how to have time with you around this work thing.

I wake early and we read on the living room couch before your father rises. I breastfeed you in the morning, the evening, and multiple times in the darkness of the night.

I soak up every second.

Having time to myself, I realize, has made me a better mother.

I am able to bring home other parts of the world to you. I'm more dynamic. I have more patience with you.

You also get affection from and experiences with your dad and his friends and their kids, and I am so happy about that because I don't have everything to give. I'm just one mortal with one set of experiences and the specific knowledge I've come to acquire. I'm flawed and lacking, and that's okay—because there are others in this world for you to learn from. There are others to love you.

LETTING GO

Spring

I miss my daughter's babyhood already. In her growing up I have watched the present become the past, have seen at first hand how life acquires the savour of longing....

It is incredible to me—who remembers the oneness, the image on the snowy screen of her two-inch-long body lying in my darkness, as if it were yesterday, as if it were still there—that our joinedness for her is such a distant state.

—Rachel Cusk, *A Life's Work*

You are ten months old, baby. This seems like a leap in the story, but that's how it goes with you babies—suddenly you are ten months, two years, a teenager.

Enjoy it! It goes so fast! coo the mothers of older children, while I'm here in the thick of it.

Yes, I can see how there has been so much in this little time, how rapidly you've changed. I swear you were nothing but warm, blinking flesh just the other day and now you can stand, eat bananas, try words.

You are edging your way out of my perimeter. You have two bruises on your forehead because you love to shimmy your way around our coffee table, lurch for any surface in reach, head for stairs or open cupboards, put random objects in your mouth. Sometimes, you fall, you fail. We let you have adventures while keeping you safe—it's a tricky balance. I am there, waiting, my breath held, wanting to let you explore and tensed against the potential danger, poised to catch you but hoping to not interfere unnecessarily. Remember when you were safe in my arms?

As I watch these minor tumbles, I am aware of how much pain and joy are still in store for you, and that I don't know which you'll have more of.

South African Philosopher David Benatar asserts that giving life is unethical because it is "permeated by badness," not just due to the potential for trauma and pain, but the amount of time we spend feeling uncomfortable, frustrated, lonely, or irritated. In his book, *The Human Predicament: A Candid Guide to Life's Biggest Questions*, he says that even if we believe our lives are happy, we still spend most of our time in discomfort—we're cold or hot, we have to pee, we're hungry, we're tired but can't nap—or we're grieving (over any type of loss). We have menstrual cramps or allergies, are stuck waiting in line or waiting in traffic. Our lives, he says, are characterized by a string of "frustrations and irritations."

He doesn't think any of the joy we experience measures up.

Watching you, I must disagree with him. I see all the wonder and all the joy you experience at doing life and I think this must be worth it.

But maybe that is just a necessary illusion. Your world is still so small. Over time, you will be exposed to and/or learn more and more about our species' cruelty, horror, and grief. War, famine, death, racism, injustice, betrayal, misogyny, poverty, violence, homophobia, disease, loss. The list goes on. For some people, childhood, especially early childhood, is a brief respite from these horrors, if they're lucky. And then you grow up.

It doesn't all just get worse though, Jude, there are trade-offs: in return, you will hopefully experience friendship, romantic love, good sex, travel, achievement, passion.

You always trade one thing for another.

Could I measure my own joy and pain and decide the balance?

✿

I think *you* have tipped the balance.

✿

The light of you when I return from work, your eyes bright with life.

✿

Is it enough that I don't know if your life will be worth living, but that I believe it will be, and I will do my best to make it that way? Is that forgivable?

We decide to sleep train you around this time. I never thought I'd do this. I thought I wouldn't be able to stomach it.

But you've been waking up every single hour for milk for the past two months. It is too much to bear. The world has started to dim. I want sleep, Jude. I want to feel normal. It's been a long time since I've felt normal.

We've tried gentle methods of sleep training and nothing has worked, so I eventually decide to try one of the various cry-it-out methods I've read about in parenting books. With the method I choose, I sit near your crib and leave you to cry when you wake up in the middle of the night wanting to eat; this is supposed to teach you to soothe yourself back to sleep. I sit in a chair in the dark and watch you and just let you cry and cry. I don't move toward you, but occasionally I gave a sound or word of comfort, which, given your level of distress, does not help at all.

When you cry, it yanks at me, sends my cortisol flooding. Every fiber of my being wants to pick you up and hold you against my chest, smother you with kisses. My muscles are tense and I'm practically holding my breath.

The fact that I don't rescue you, that I sit here and watch you for forty-five minutes one night, twenty the next, and so on, is proof of my desperate need for sleep. I hate doing this, but I also know I deserve to be able to take pleasure in life again, which absolutely requires sleep.

This idea I deserve pleasure, even as your mother and at the cost of your temporary discomfort, strikes me as a radical notion requiring firm confidence in these weeks.

On the first night of this training, my mother is visiting. I've warned her that she needs to ignore your crying, hoping her bed on the lower floor will protect her from the worst, but after you cry for forty minutes at three a.m. that first night, she bursts in and says, *I don't care what the goddamned book says, pick up the baby!*

I refuse. We have a standoff and I explain how desperate I am. Your poor grandmother. I'm not mad—I get it. She knows this is hard for you and she knows this is hard for me. She wants to save us.

She goes back downstairs. Your dad, in bed in the room adjacent, is amused. He's not sitting in here because he thinks our presence will only make it worse, like why let you see I am just sitting there while you cry? I'm not sure, baby, I guess I want you to know I haven't abandoned you entirely.

The literature on sleep training is mixed. Some of it tells me this type of training is essential for giving you the skill of being able to fall asleep on your own, and that the benefits of a good night's sleep outweigh any sense of neglect it might impart to you at this age.

Other books and blogs tell me this is cruel and unnatural. They tell me I am teaching you I'm not there for you, teaching you to give up on me, and that on the night when you finally stop crying for me, it is simply because you wake up and realize you can't count on me anymore. I feel pain considering this. Then I feel furious. Not there for you?! I am there for you ten billion times during the hours of six a.m. and eight p.m.

And if I sleep, I can show up for you in a way I couldn't if I were sleep-deprived. I can be more engaged, more attentive, and more playful when I am well-rested. I am willing to go on more adventures with you.

This is another one of those impossible choices in motherhood. Either way, someone could fault me.

After a few days of this, you sleep through the night, essentially every night, from then on.

In the mornings, you stand eagerly at the bars of your crib, calling for us. You smile with your gums, eyes glinting, challenging your dad and me to the day.

You have long hair now. We occasionally put barrettes in it to keep it out of your eyes and some of our extended family members are mortified at how it—as one puts it—*instantly transforms you into a girl.*

Barrettes or none, when we're in public many people do mistake you for a girl, perhaps because we dress you in all sorts of colors, or because of that long hair, or because there's little difference in children this young and if you remove or swap those signifiers—the long hair, the colors, then you are, in a sense, instantly another gender.

I don't understand why it's so important to us adults to know the gender of the children we are speaking to. Is it so we know how to act around them? How to talk to them?

And how is that exactly?

When people in public do mistake you for a girl, they tell you how pretty your outfit is. They call you a princess. When they think you're a boy, they comment on how big you are or what a good appetite you have.

When they think you're a girl, there's such a softness, such a commotion over your preciousness.

You play with all sorts of things. You have a dollhouse with min-iature dolls in it and you like to open and close it and put them in-side. You also have a large doll my parents brought from a trip to England, dressed all in pink. You love her. You carry her around. You try to share your bottle with her. You get distressed when her tiny pink hat comes off.

You also love playing with blocks and your kitchen set, any-thing else with doors that open and close, and containers and measuring spoons.

What you don't really like are trucks, yet people keep buy-ing them for you. It doesn't really matter who you are, it matters you're a boy, and people buy trucks for boys. They sit in the gar-den unused and eventually I donate them, only to receive more.

My baby, the world is going to make you love or pretend to love them.

I really want you to stay you, and that is all I am trying to do—give you all the options and let you choose.

I didn't expect the clothes we dress you in and the toys we allow you to play with to be such a big deal. It seems to be important to many people to signal their children's sex from early on. I'm always baffled by the headbands with big bows that parents will put on their infant daughters—they're pure decoration, pure signifiers. Perhaps I understand better the desire to exclaim one's pride over having a girl in this way—a way of saying, *I value that she is a girl because girls are awesome* in a world that is still misogynistic.

I want boys to be able to have rainbows and sparkle, too, if they want it, because what child wouldn't be attracted to all that? I want femininity to be valued.

In the boys' section at the store: sports, camo, tough guy T-shirts, loose fit.

Wandering over to the girls'—everything is skin-tight, pink, sparkling. *Daddy's princess* say the T-shirts.

If I was the mother of a daughter, I think I would be angry a lot.

Your dad's parental leave is ending.

We scramble to find you a day care. We've been on a city list for day care centers since I was pregnant, but apparently that wasn't early enough. None of the centers have spaces. Another mother tells me she got on the list when she started trying to conceive—*Didn't I know about this?!* she asks. One friend says it is all about calling and calling the centers and making them like you so that you can jump the queue. We're not good at doing this.

As a result of our apparent slackerness, we resort to home day care.

Eventually, we find a woman named Eleanor who has a spot in her home care. We call her references, who speak of her glowingly. She has a wonderful way with the kids already in her care, and your dad and I both get a good feeling about her, but it is still terrifying to leave you to a stranger, all day, every day.

It fills my belly with dread. It's one thing to have you at home with your father and another thing for you to be entirely out of our sphere.

But you are almost twelve months old now. This is what I am supposed to do, or what we planned to do, or what I want to do. Sort of.

I want to work. I also don't want to work—I want to be with you. I feel guilty, I feel angry about feeling guilty.

I feel superstitious.

Mothers get punished, that's all I know, for wanting their own lives. For careers. For putting anything ahead of their children, even for a second. You don't get to have a baby and not sacrifice yourself to the child every second for the rest of your life.

Right?

I start having the thought that mothering is a slow losing.

Your love starts off so immense, Jude, seems almost equal to mine (though nothing could be), and it will slowly dim until I am just another asshole in a world full of them. Just an asshole who loves you more than anyone else does. One day, you'll realize that.

I hope you forgive me for this sleight of hand, this card trick, and hold space for some tenderness.

I hope I can always be someone you believe in. I will always work toward that.

I'm getting way ahead of myself, as always. It is simply the first day of day care, you are not leaving us or moving away. I take this shift hard though—it is the end of your babyhood.

Your father, as always, is cool and collected. I'm a wreck.

You cry every morning when we drop you off, wanting us, confused. Eleanor is gentle and loving, and I am so glad you are going to be with other children, but I feel like I've betrayed you.

Each day for your entire first week there, I expect a phone call saying you've had an accident and died. It's irrational. Sometimes motherhood is like that.

Eventually, my anxiety dissipates when each day you return alive. Eventually, you stop crying. Eventually, you grow to love day care and I realize Eleanor is probably a better "parent" than we are in a lot of ways. Calmer, more organized, more experienced, and better at setting boundaries. We're just two people who had a baby, while she chose this as a career path. In other words, she knows what she's doing and we're still just figuring it out.

In the evenings, your father can no longer give me a rundown of your day. Your life is a mystery.

This is your first independent venture into the world. You are becoming more of a person—your own person. When I let go of my worry, I realize it's amazing and I'm proud of you—you becoming. I'm excited even, to watch you grow in the world without me.

I want other people to show you all the ways there are to be human.

It was temporary, baby, the way you took my life hostage. Why couldn't I see that until recently?

I'm getting bits of my self back, even if they are changed.

In some ways, this year was like a deconstruction.

Now I decide how I put myself back together again.

I don't want to pretend that motherhood has magically changed me into a better person, but it has pushed me into a constant striving to be worthy of the generous way you view me. I am more patient through sheer necessity, and calmer for the same reason—it feels essential to parenting you.

My self-loathing has softened. When the urge arises, I tamp it down, wanting to protect both you and my own inner child from it. As I stop feeding the voice, it gets smaller. I could and should have done this before you, but I don't think I felt I had reason to.

I hope you are kinder to yourself than I have ever been to mine.

I was so unprepared for motherhood. I also know now there is no preparing.

All the days were so long, baby. Sometimes excruciatingly so, but the year has bolted past me. All of it—you—like a stunning warping of time.

It is like yesterday, but also forever ago, that you were fresh from my body, your tiny, clenched limbs, blue eyes turning up to me.

The first time you smiled. Cooed. Laughed. Rolled over. Crawled.

The look on your face when you tasted solid food at six months, as if you'd been waiting for that mouthful your entire short life.

Your first word. Not mama, not dada, but *light*, which you pronounce "ight."

Each piece of becoming so small but achieving something so big.

You are one year old.

I am a mother.

As we celebrate your first birthday, I experience a phenomenon that other moms had told me about but that I'd never experienced until now: mourning for previous versions of you.

Newborn you and four-month-old you and six-month-old you and nine-month-old you.

I have permanently lost the person you were at those stages and the rapid rate of your development makes me aware I am quickly losing the person you are today.

What's stranger is that you will not recall any of the moments I have shared with you along the way, any moments from this entire messy, brilliant, devastating year—your memory does not keep them at these ages.

My grief over all of this is sweeping, undoes me. I realize I have given you—and will continue to give you—so much, without knowing how or if you will use it.

Without knowing what will happen to you.

Without knowing if you will enjoy or even survive the things that come at you in this life.

I can't do anything about that.

But I *can* endure the overwhelming uncertainty of all that, the vulnerability of mothering, even if it can feel impossible. It is the price I pay for having intimately known your small being from the second you entered this world, for experiencing you becoming a person, for helping guide you in becoming. I am willing to be raw with love and grief for this.

You have taught me that vulnerability is all. It is where everything stunning and worthwhile happens.

I will continue to give, Jude, continue to love you, and at some point, I'll just let go—like I did under the water that day in California, knowing only that the sky is above or below me, and that you're there, too, swirling in the ocean beside me.

Do women like that make good mothers? I'd like to know.

ACKNOWLEDGMENTS

I would like to thank the people who kept me afloat during the long, sleep-deprived years I spent writing this. To Brecken Hancock, who gave valuable feedback on a very early draft, constantly encouraged me, and shared many conversations with me that helped inform this book. I'm so grateful to have your company in writing and mothering. To my grandmother, Shirley, for opening up about pregnancy and childbirth in a different era and for always speaking up for women. To my mom, Barb, for fact-checking family histories and allowing me to share sensitive parts of her life. To my dad, Paul, for always supporting me. To both for always encouraging my writing, even though, to quote Doireann Ní Ghríofa, "it cannot be easy to bear the embarrassment of a writer in the family." To my mother-in-law, Debbie, for giving me time to write and for her support over the years. To Andrew, for being an adoring uncle. To Clay, for enthusiasm and understanding, for reading and loving countless versions of this, for persistence.

To the friends who kept asking me about this project and took the time to read early drafts and provide feedback: Linda Besner, Amica Hewitt, Ben Ladouceur, Wes Marskell, and

Rebecca Rappeport. To Harriett Alida Lye, for reminding me to include my mother. To my former agent, Stephanie Sinclair, who was an early believer in *Motherlike* and whose encouragement was crucial. To my editor, Allison LaSorda, who helped me fill in the gaps. To my agent, Paige Sisley, for guidance. To Brenda Williams, for always checking in. To Laurie Newman, whose mothering and reading inspire me.

To the team at Second Story Press: thank you for believing in this book. To Jordan Ryder, who ushered me through the editorial process with such grace and attention to detail. To Emma Rodgers and the whole marketing team for all they do. To Laura Atherton for rendering it such an elegant object, and to Jessica Sullivan for designing a cover that speaks loudly.

I'm also grateful for the financial support provided by the Ontario Arts Council.

And to my children, who have each made a piece of this mother. To Jude, who taught me so much about myself and the world as I became his mom, whose intelligence and creativity continue to dazzle me. To Elton, whose delightful silliness and profoundly loving nature sustained me during the grittiest part of writing this. *I've never seen such devotion in a droid.* To Ambrose, who blazed into this world not long ago, bringing so much sweetness. I can't wait to see you become. To all three of you: I hope one day you can read this without cringing too much, having been raised with the knowledge your mother is also a woman.

Finally, this work wouldn't be what it is without all the mothers whose stories or words I share in these pages; I am profoundly grateful to all of you.

ABOUT THE AUTHOR

Katherine Leyton's collection of poetry, *All the Gold Hurts My Mouth*, won the 2017 ReLit Award, was shortlisted for an Ottawa Book Award, and received a starred review in *Publishers Weekly*. Born and raised in Toronto, Katherine has also worked as a screenwriter and has been nominated for a National Magazine Award for her nonfiction, which has appeared in the *Globe and Mail*, *Bitch*, *This Magazine*, and *Arc*, among others.